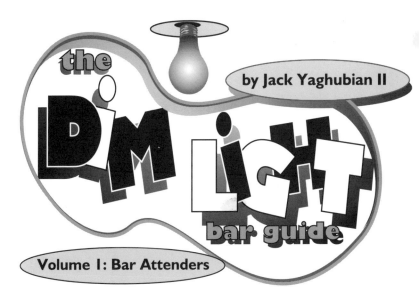

the Dim Light bar guide

by Jack Yaghubian II

Volume 1: Bar Attenders

"You want to get drunk, I want to make money— let's party!" – J.Y.

POP-CULT PUBLISHING

Pop-cult Publishing   San Francisco California USA

Yaghubian, Jack Hagop II, 1949–
Dim Light Bar Guide: volume 1/ Jack Yaghubian — 1st ed.

ISBN 0-9667119-0-4 (pb)

All illustrations in this book are by *Fast, Cheap & Easy Graphics* and are copyrighted by same. Illustrations at the beginning of each chapter are details from a larger work entitled *Barnica*.

Thanks to World Litho Services for Film Output and Production Consultation.
Printed in Hong Kong by Colorcraft Ltd.

This book is dedicated to my friend, Tim Yohannon, the founder and publisher of Maximum Rock & Roll magazine who died of cancer earlier this year. He was a good friend and a man of principle until the end. He was also the best damned Risk player (that's right...the board game) I ever faced on the board of honor.

Table of Contents

Table of Contents

Author's Note

About two years ago, as I leaned against the back bar smoking a cigarette, I made the decision to write this book. As I recall, it was after midnight on a Monday and business had slowed to a crawl. I surveyed the bar before me: an empty highball glass with a puddle of bar sweat at it's base pleaded to be bussed. I considered it but decided to wait until I'd finished my smoke. A little further down the bar sat two women, discussing the merits of their favorite form of exercise between sips of lemon drops. Next to them sat the cocktail waitress, passing the time by chatting with a male customer.

Earlier things hadn't been so calm. I'd stood in the same spot but, rather than reclining, I whirled like a dervish, snatching glasses, scooping ice, grabbing bottles, taking money and making change. As I finished with one customer another would pop up in her place. Behind that customer was another and another. They swarmed three deep around the bar, shouting orders and yelling "Hey! Bartender! Bartender!" I was in the weeds and I knew it.

My thoughts at the time were, 'these people don't know what the hell they're doing.' Their only hard knowledge seemed to be that they wanted to get drunk and a bar was the place to do it. Beyond that simple set of facts, they were oblivious. In short, I was doing my job but they weren't doing theirs. If they were, they would get their drinks faster and my work would be both easier and more lucrative.

Later, the dust finally settled, and I let my mind wander as I smoked. My thoughts brought me to an idea I'd first had years earlier; to write a book on how to order, pay and tip. I had never seriously considered writing it, I just used it as a conversation piece with other bar workers who always agreed that such a book was needed. Secretly, I wished that one of these bartenders or cocktail waitresses would get enthused and write a book of their own on the subject. I was always otherwise occupied, or maybe just too lazy to start the project myself.

But on this night, which had been such an unnecessary chore, I decided that since no one else had written it, I had to. After all, how hard could it be? At the time, I envisioned it as a small pamphlet that could be photocopied and given away.

Now, two years later, here I sit with the project near completion. It has since grown beyond the pamphlet scale. My publisher has elected to split it into two small books: Volume one, which deals with information for the bar customer, is the book you hold in your hand. Volume two, which describes the job of bartending is due to be released in the spring of 2000.

My credentials for writing these books, while not as impressive as many in the business, include twelve years of bartending and over thirty years of bar attending. While my bartending experience has been confined to the city limits of San Francisco, I believe the gist of what I have to say on the subject is applicable far beyond the limits of this small city. Whether I'm an "expert" or not is a moot point, because as far as I can tell, if you want to read a book on this subject, I'm the only game in town.

In closing I would like to thank my publisher, Pop-cult Publishing for taking a chance with my oddball book and to it's parent company, Fast, Cheap & Easy Graphics which not only OK'd the deal but did all the graphics, design, and layout work.

I would also like to thank all of the bartenders, bar owners, bar managers, bar backs, cocktail waitresses and doormen I've worked with and learned from over the years and the many customers, from the sublime to the beligerated, whom I've served and there by made my living, lo these many years.

I'd also like to thank my proof reader, Michael Bejbl, who was a customer of mine for several years, during which time he earned the nickname *Basil Hayden* due to his love for a bourbon by that name.

And I want to thank my editor Nicolette Dalpino, who works in a shop near my apartment and whose grandparents ran a bar. Her insight into the bar business and her knowledge of the English language did much to make this a readable work.

Jack Yaghubian 1998 San Francisco, CA.

PART 1

the Basics

Bartenders are just legal-drug dealers.

➤**Know what you want before you get the bartender's (BT's) attention.** This is especially important when the bar is very busy or *slammed*.

➤**Give your entire order at once.** Don't break it up into a string of mini-orders.

➤**Name booze first when ordering.** A "vodka-cranberry" rather than "cranberry-vodka." This will speed up the process by giving the BT information in the order in which it will be used. For example, when making a drink that calls for mixer, the BT pours the booze first, then finishes with mixer. In this way you will also avoid confusion with cranberry-infused vodka.

The same goes for *call* liquor, "Stoli martini," or "Tanqueray-tonic." If you don't call your liquor you will get what is in the well—generally the cheapest stuff with names you don't recognize.

If you want your drink *tall* mention this first, say, "Tall vodka-cranberry." If you don't the BT may have already filled a high-ball glass with ice and will have to start over.

► **When with a group designate one person to both order and pay.** No bartender wants to have five people come up to the bar and have to deal with them one at a time. An added advantage to this method of ordering is that you can tip less per drink. BTs expect a larger percentage on drinks ordered individually.

► **Have your money out when the drinks arrive.** This may be sooner than you think, so it's best to have your money ready at the time you order.

► **Pay with the largest bill** or combination of bills that will cover the order. Don't wait until the BT tells you what you owe and then start looking through every bill in your wallet for the closest combination of bills.

► **Don't toss a crumpled pile of bills on the bar as your payment.**

► **Avoid using coins.** If forced to use coins, don't use anything smaller than a quarter. Bars don't use nickels, dimes and pennies. If you do, you'll just annoy the BT.

► **Don't place your order and walk away.** The BT can usually produce the drinks faster than you imagine and will be standing there wondering where you've gone by the time you return from the restroom or talking with friends. As soon as you place your order you should be reaching for your wallet, if your money isn't already out.

Ordering & Paying

➤**When placing a large order, don't start picking up drinks and ferrying them to your friends before the BT has completed your order unless you first ask the BT if it's okay to do so.**

➤**When to say "Thank you."** A mistake some customers make is to thank the BT upon tendering an amount of money from which they are expecting change. Generally, when a customer says "Thank you" the implication is that the transaction is complete—no change is expected. In a "friendly" bar this shouldn't pose a problem; the BT will realize that you're just not familiar with the conventions of ordering and paying in a bar. However, in high-volume bars and clubs, where the clientele is largely anonymous, a customer who thanks the BT prematurely may get a "Thank yoooou!" instead of the expected change.

➤**Cash is always better than credit cards.** Credit card transactions cost both the owner and the BT money.

 Credit cards slow things down because the BT is required to make notes each time a new round of drinks is ordered. When it comes time to settle the bill, more time is lost. When the bar is slammed, this results in fewer drinks being served.

 Another concern is stolen credit cards. Unless the BT confirms each card when the tab is opened, the bar could be be dealing with a stolen card. The BTs choice is to take the time to confirm the card or take the chance that at the end of the night the bar is left holding a bad card against which the customer has rung up a large tab and then walked.

 Even with legitimate credit card transactions there is an added cost to the owner in the form of being paid by the credit company several weeks later, with a percentage charged for carrying the credit. In addition to this, customers will sometimes forget that they have a card at the bar and walk out without closing it. They usually return, though not always, and even when they do it may not be for a week, so payment from the credit company is delayed further.

From the BT's perspective there is another big negative to credit card transactions: there is no way to know if they are dealing with a stiff when they run a credit card. For all the BT knows there will be a big goose egg on the tip line when the card is closed. Cash eliminates these problems.

➤**Cash is better than tabs.** Like credit cards, tabs slow things down and present a greater opportunity for scams.

➤**Checks.** Approximately 50% of all bad checks passed in the U.S. are passed in bars. For this reason BTs generally won't take a check unless they know the customer very well. Even then they prefer small checks because, if the above statements are true, then it follows that regulars bounce checks too.

➤**Traveler's checks.** Most bars will accept these if they're being used to pay for drinks, though they may require a picture I.D. Generally, twenty-dollar traveler's checks are preferred to fifty or one-hundred-dollar denominations.

➤**Specify variations.** For example, a vodka martini. A regular martini is gin and vermouth chilled, served up in a martini glass with olives. Many people order a martini when what they really want is a *vodka* martini. Most BTs will ask to be sure, but if you order a martini and the BT starts to work, unless it's a BT who knows what you drink, you can expect gin.

➤**Call liquor.** If you want a screwdriver made with Stoli, say so up front, "I want a Stoli screwdriver." Occasionally, a customer will watch a BT pour a screwdriver, and then ask, "Don't you have Stoli?"

7

Of course, the BT has Stoli, but if the customer doesn't ask for it, it's assumed to be a well drink.

►**Special instructions.** The custom-made drink, or drinks so far out of the ordinary that few people have ever heard of them. If you know what you're doing this is fine, but expect some variation. The way to order special drinks is by 'parts' per ingredient. Don't tell the BT the amounts, "a shot of gin, a shot of Kahlua," etc. Customers who do this generally don't know what they're talking about, and end up describing a drink that costs a small fortune. The proper way to order is this: "Three parts gin, one part Kahlua, one part Chambord, chilled, up with a cherry" (to describe what I expect would be an especially nasty drink). This tells the BT everything he needs to know: it's a drink based on gin with the flavors of coffee and raspberry. It's a martini pour (two ounces of booze rather than one and a half). It's chilled then strained into a martini glass and it gets a cherry garnish.

►**Have a second choice.** If you have only the vaguest idea of the ingredients, it's better to order something else. In such cases, the BT can only go by your description. If it sounds really odd, the BT will tell you, but some exotic drinks do have odd combinations of ingredients. Once the drink is made, that's it. Most BTs will replace it if you don't like it, but then you've wasted their time and the boss's booze.

The fact is, no bartender knows all the drinks in all the books, not to mention the ones that are of recent invention and not published. Another fact is that it's not to a BT's financial advantage to know more than a small fraction of all the possible drinks, because few people are going to order them. Those who do order drinks that are way out of the norm are usually

How to Get What You Want

people who don't go to bars very often, which means they probably don't tip very well, if at all. This means BTs have little incentive to remember obscure drink recipes, combine all the ingredients, then try to figure out what to charge. If it's really slow and there's no other work to do, it can be a diversion, but that's the best that can be said on the subject.

►**Regional differences.** While on vacation it's good to keep in mind that different regions of the world have different tastes. What's preferred in some regions will be rare or unknown in others.

For instance, I've had Spanish customers order red wine and Coke. I've served Galliano on the rocks to an English woman. When Europeans order a martini, what they are probably expecting is Martini & Rossi Vermouth on the rocks. Some Englishmen like 7-Up in their beer. Europeans in general don't like ice in their drinks. The Irish prefer Miller Genuine Draft above all other beers.

Garnishes vary from place to place. For example, in California a rum-and-Coke doesn't call for a lime unless asked for (a rum-and-coke with a lime is known as a "Cuba-libre"). I was informed by a woman from Connecticut that rum-and-coke always gets a lime where she comes from. On the other hand, in the United States a gin-and-tonic always gets a lime, though my English customers prefer lemon. In California, tequila is usually not taken with a garnish but if it is, it's taken with salt and lime. Customers visiting from the East Coast generally prefer salt and lemon.

Some people like their stout at room temperature, others like a lemon wedge in their wheat beer. These people are Americans who have been to Europe. While I assume they exist, I have never encountered an Irish customer who asked me for warm stout and when I have offered a lemon wedge in wheat beer to Germans or Belgians, nine times out of ten they have declined it, often with a puzzled look in my direction.

➤**Amateur hour drinks.** These are drinks that tell the BT that you don't drink very often. They include just about anything that comes out of a blender or that calls for a small paper umbrella. They also indicate to the BT that the tip is going to be small or nonexistent.

➤**Fru Fru drinks.** Closely related to Amateur hour drinks. Generally, people ordering these drinks do spend a good deal of time in bars, they just don't like the taste of alcohol and/or aren't very sophisticated drinkers. Fru Fru drinks can be recognized by the fact that they are often sweet, call for three or more ingredients and have cute names like "Dead Elvis," "Alabama Slammer," or "Blue Hawaiian."

➤**Fad liquors.** Liquors that come into fashion for a couple of years due to savvy marketing techniques. These are usually relatively low-quality products that depend on false claims such as, "It has opiates in it, the government will be making it illegal soon," which was the case with Jagermeister, or gimmicks like the addition of a few pennies worth of gold leaf to an otherwise ordinary bottle of booze like Gold Schlager.

➤**House specials.** Usually some concoction the management has dreamed up to sell to suckers; cheap booze mixed with all sorts of crap and sold at greater than normal markup, which is already considerable in a bar.

➤**Extra strong.** I have found over the years that people who ask for their drinks "extra strong" are likely to be *stiffs*. Consequently, they get nothing extra from me; more often they get less. It's a simple matter to pack the glass extra tight with ice so there's less room for liquid. It will look fuller, and if it's a drink that calls for filler a splash will fill it and the drink will taste stronger, even though it contains no more than a shot of booze. If I get stiffed I simply short-pour him on the next round and add even less filler. It's also possible to short-pour and add a float of booze at the end. This makes the customer think you're adding extra booze, and when he takes his first sip it will taste strong because the float will be on top and all he'll taste is booze.

➤**Less ice.** Some people will order their highballs with less ice or no ice thinking that the BT will make up for the lost volume by adding more booze. This is a classic rookie move. The BT

What Not to Order

will give you a half-full highball. If you complain that it's not full she'll then fill it with mixer, not booze.

➤**Shooters.** I don't recommend shooters. I think it's a dumb way to drink. Usually sweet concoctions with "naughty" names so that amateurs can think that they're getting down with their bad selves. Give me a break!

➤**Poppers.** A dumb way to drink plus soda pop.

➤**Anything found in a drink menu.** Drink menus are strictly for bush-league drinkers.

➤**Stumping the BT.** Some people seem to believe that if they order a drink the BT hasn't heard of, he will be impressed with their knowledge. This simply isn't true. The impression the BT receives from such an order is that he's dealing with a novice drinker.

➤**Wine.** If you're a wine connoisseur, you might want to think about ordering something else in a bar. Most bars will have a small selection of wine, and they don't take care of their wine as you would like. In my experience, wine lovers are often disappointed by the wine they get in a bar.

Occasionally, I'm asked why we don't have a better selection of wine, and why we open bottles and let them sit. The answer to the second question is that when someone orders a glass of wine the BT wants to be able to pour it as quickly as possible. Rather than stopping to open a bottle when slammed, BTs often open one or more bottles in advance.

Not a Good Idea to Order

The answer to the first question is that the more choices you offer, the more bottles you will have opened, and the greater the chance that someone will send the wine back because it's been open too long for their taste.

Wine drinkers are just too finicky to be accommodated. You will never have a gin-and-tonic sent back because the bottle has been open too long. The way I've come to deal with this over the years is that when a customer asks me if I have "a nice wine," I always say "no, I don't." The tipoff is the word "nice"; this tells me that they're likely to be fussy, so I avoid the problem altogether. They usually appreciate this, and it's good for the boss too; it does him no good for me to pour a glass of wine down the drain and replace it with a vodka-tonic. I serve them the vodka-tonic in the first place and save time and/or expense for everyone concerned.

▶**Bloody Marys after five in the afternoon.** Bloody Marys are a morning or an afternoon drink. You can order them at night, but you're showing the BT and the other customers that you don't know what you're doing.

▶**Long Island Iced Tea.** A little bit of everything, so it tastes like nothing. A drink for the college crowd, but if you're over 25, it's a bit silly.

▶**Jell-O shots.** Can it get any more juvenile than this?

▶**Coffee.** Bars are not cafes. Coffee is a small sideline used to wake up the bar staff, sober up the drunks, and make Irish coffees and other coffee-based drinks. Because of this, bar-coffee tends to be of low quality and is often stale. When the BT makes a pot it will sit until it's finished, which may be several hours later.

For coffee drinks this is fine, because the quality

Not a Good Idea to Order

of the coffee and it's staleness will be masked by the booze. For its other main uses, waking up staff and sobering up drunks, it will also do fine, because the former just want the caffeine and the latter are not likely to be too discriminating about the taste of their coffee. But as coffee goes, it won't be very good. Keep this in mind if you have a desire for a Cup of Joe as you pass a bar; it might be wiser to continue down the street until you find a cafe where they make their living selling coffee.

➤**Espresso.** Considering the above, espresso may seem like a good idea. Many bars these days have espresso machines and as espresso is made on the spot, you know it will be fresh and relatively strong. However, you will also find that most BTs have little interest in making espresso and probably aren't very good at it. Consequently, the espresso they make is not likely to be very good.

➤**Cappuccino.** An even worse bet, as BTs hate making them. The reason for this is that a cappuccino takes three times longer to make than a gin-and-tonic but costs less and commands a smaller tip. The BT will make about 25% as much for making a cappuccino as for making a drink. Then there's the "copycat" order; someone sees you order a cappuccino and thinks, "gee, that looks like a good idea," and pretty soon the BT becomes an unwilling barrista. If you want an espresso or a cappuccino, go to a café.

Ideally, you should order drinks that you enjoy. You will find, however, that sophisticated drinkers will often deride sweet drinks, drinks with cute names or lots of ingredients, and drinks that come out of a blender or require excessive garnishes. You may object to this, after all it's just a matter of taste and you happen to like sweet drinks. But if that's the case, have you ever found yourself in an argument over the comparative merits of cheap, sweet, cherry-flavored wine vs. fine, aged cabernet? This is the way sophisticated drinkers view all those sweet, creamy, fruity drinks festooned with gratuitous garnishes; it's kid stuff. If you want to order like an adult drinker, here are some tips:

What the Regulars Order

➤**Regular drinkers always drink the same drink**, they rarely hop from one drink to another. Occasionally they will have something out of the ordinary; perhaps they have several alternate drinks, depending on their mood, or they feel like trying something new, but they rarely have more than two different types of drinks during a drinking session.

➤**Regular drinkers keep to drinks that have no more than two primary ingredients.** For example; beer, gin and tonic, Jim Beam over, martinis, etc.

➤ **Ordering neat.** If you want to try some liquor that you have never had before, order it *neat* with a water back and alternate between sips of booze and water. This way you will be able to taste it and decide if it's something you like.

➤**If drinking neat shots of booze experienced drinkers rarely shoot it.** They sip it. If you shoot booze it usually means you don't like the taste; drinkers like the taste of booze.

➤**As a rule of thumb, the plainer the bottle, the simpler the label, and the more unfamiliar the name, the better the beverage inside.** For instance, if I'm in a liquor store and confronted by two bottles of red wine that cost the same, I always pick the one with the simplest label. Also, it's best to avoid bottles shaped like people or animals, that look as if they were specially designed to stand out on the shelf, or that come in anything other than clear, green or brown glass bottles. If you're in the mood for cognac and you see Hennessey, Remy Martin or Couvoisier on the shelf, and next to that you see something in an ordinary bottle with a name you don't recognize, that's the good stuff. I'd advise asking the price before you order it.

➤**Why.** Tipping is customary in the United States in many service industries. Doormen, bellhops, waiters/waitresses, and bartenders are the primary occupations that expect and depend on tips. Tips are an important component of the incomes of taxi drivers, beauticians, and hotel maids (among others), but it is the first group for whom tips account for over half of their income.

Besides this, BTs generally do not receive benefits such as paid vacations, healthcare, or even sick pay; in fact, missing a shift for any reason, including illness, without getting someone to cover your shift, is grounds for dismissal. For these reasons,

Tipping

BTs depend heavily on tips. If not for tips, most BTs working today would be forced to leave the profession for financial reasons. Those who stayed would find their incomes reduced by over 50 percent.

Those drawn to the void left by the departed would be the same people drawn to other low-paying jobs. I have no doubt that they could perform all the tasks necessary to make a drink and the other incidental tasks required of the job, but the quality of service would suffer and the social aspect would disappear. Without the incentive of tips there would be little motivation for the new bar employees so the owners would have to improve their bottom line in other ways. Eventually bars would deteriorate to very utilitarian affairs.

Visiting one of these hypothetical bars, somewhere in a future where tipping is no longer customary, the first thing you notice is that there's a lot of singing and talking going on but there's somethings amiss. The talking isn't in the form of conversation, but rather bursts of disjointed speech. The singing starts, then stops, here, then there and no one is singing the same song.

As you approach the bar, instead of a bartender there's what appears to be a bored store clerk behind it. As you take a seat at the bar he makes no effort to approach you. Instead he stares blankly over your head. After waiting several uncomfortable minutes for him to notice you, you realize that he is watching one of several silent T.V.s mounted on the wall behind you. You make a few subtle gestures to get his attention but finally, in frustration, you wave your arms in his line of sight. Suddenly, he smiles and approaches. You begin to ask for a gin-and-tonic, but instead of taking your order he hands you a booklet, then steps back and resumes staring at one of the screens.

The booklet, which is entitled *The Micro-Bucks Drinking Experience,* turns out to be an extensive listing of all the beer, wine, booze and mixed drinks offered by the bar. Each drink listed is accompanied by a glowing account of it's characteristics. Prices are listed in neat rows across from each entry followed by an arcane group of numbers and letters.

You page through the booklet and eventually find gin-and-tonic. Again you must work to get the clerks attention. He waits for a break in the programming, then with an annoyed look, he turns to the first page of the booklet and points to instructions on ordering and paying. It instructs you to insert a debit card into the slot on the bar in front of your seat and then to type in the code number for the drink you selected on one of the many membrane keyboards that line the bar.

After doing as instructed, a plastic cup pops out of one of several chutes on the otherwise unadorned backbar and a precise amount of booze, ice and mixer is deposited into it from a spout positioned just above the plastic cup. Without averting his gaze, the clerk reaches around to grab the cup and places it on the bar in front of you.

Now, leaning back in your chair to enjoy your drink you begin to notice your surroundings. The guy sitting to your right is wearing a headset. Occasionally, he makes a comment in the direction of one of the T.V.'s above the backbar. He types at a furious pace on his keyboard, turning from one T.V. to another. He tosses off the remaining brown liquid in his cup and puts it on the bar. There's a clinking sound behind the bar followed by a squirting sound. The clerk plucks a full cup

Tipping

from below the chute where it has appeared and places it before the man. He then removes the empty cup and throws it in a trash can behind the bar.

To your left sits a man who's surfing the internet on his lap top which is, literally, on his lap. He hunkers over it, a strange misshapen form, blocking the screen from all view save his own. Occasionally, he looks up at the T.V. displaying swimsuit models on a beach, takes a drink and sings a phrase from some ancient heavy metal song before before hunkering down over his lap top again. As you scan the room you find it is decorated with lot's of orange vinyl, fake wood, old timey beer signs and white walls which call your attention to the lighting; it's way too bright. As you scan the rest of the room you become aware, over the din of disconnected sentences, one sided cellphone conversations, and unrelated songs, that the most despicable muzak is being piped into the room. As you turn to voice your complaint to the clerk you find that he has placed a headset and a booklet entitled *Micro-Bucks Audio Delight* on the bar in front of you. Turning to the instruction page you discover that you can access the audio portion of any of the T.V.'s in the room plus thousands of CD titles via the headset by simply typing your coded request into the same key board you used to order your drink. After inserting your debit card into the slot in the bar, you type in numbers corresponding to your music selection and soon you're happily sipping a gin-and-tonic from your plastic cup and singing out loud to *Smells Like Teen Spirit*. Turning to the man on your right, you wonder what his name is. Realizing he can't hear you and wouldn't know you were talking to him even if he could, you exclaim, "Joe, it just doesn't get any better than this!"

Fortunately, this bleak scenario is unlikely to come about. If everyone in the United States today were to conspire to never tip again, then tomorrow the bar owners would add a 20% gratuity to the price of a drink (the price increase would be in 25-cent increments, rounded up). As it stands, the decision of how much to tip is left to the customer.

What I've implied in the above statement is that the customer is a de facto employer of the BT. The bar owner is the largest single contributor to the BT's income, in the form of a monthly paycheck, but the customers as a group contribute the largest total amount, in the form of tips. If customers refuse to pay the BT's wages something has to give; either they will be forced to pay or the whole system deteriorates.

For this reason the BT will, over the course of a shift, categorize customers according to how they tip and will make sure that the good tippers will get taken care of first. You may give a good tip to a BT who cracked a joke and told you about a good restaurant nearby and made you a drink that was to your liking, but the most important result of your tip, for you, is that service will be there when you're ready to order your next round. If, on the other hand, you stiff a BT because you felt you waited too long to get served, then you will simply be setting yourself up for a longer wait on your next round. If you adhere to this practice, then eventually you won't be able to get a drink at all. The BT is in charge of the situation.

If you don't mind barhopping, or if you rarely go to bars and never have more than two drinks, you may skip the rest of this section. If you enjoy drinking in bars, learn how to tip—both for the BT's benefit and your own.

Tipping

►**How much.** This is the big question for most people who are unfamiliar with the practice. To get to the heart of the matter: BTs want to get one dollar for each drink served. You'd prefer to give nothing. The average between these two extremes is fifty cents—the lowest amount that will insure good service ("Tips," I've been told, is an acronym for "To Insure Prompt Service"). If you're tipping a quarter then you might as well be stiffing, particularly if you're drinking *call* or *top-shelf* booze. From the BT's perspective, if you're drinking good booze and leaving a small tip, you're using money that should be used for tipping to buy yourself better booze. So, if you're drinking good booze you should leave one dollar per drink, minimum. If you're drinking *well* booze you should leave fifty cents, minimum.

Another consideration is the complexity of the drinks you order. If you're ordering booze *neat,* or if you're ordering high-balls or cheap bottled beer you can get away with fifty cents per drink, or even a little less if you're ordering rounds of drinks. But if you're ordering drinks that call for three or more ingredients, *up* drinks, especially those that call for sugared rims or other such flourishes, Bloody Marys, and coffee drinks, etc., then you should tip higher.

If you'd rather go by percentages, an average tip is 20%. A low tip is 10%. Twenty-five percent is a high tip. To figure your tip quickly take 10% and work from there. For example, if the total is $7.50, then seventy-five-cents would be 10%, a low tip. A dollar-fifty would be 20%, an average tip. Two dollars or more would be a good tip. It's best to go by percentages when you enter the realm of high priced booze. For instance, if you're drinking aged, single malt scotches they will

AT YOUR SERVICE

Tipping

almost always be over five dollars a shot. A one dollar tip on an eighteen dollar shot of scotch isn't going to cut it. This is also true when you're in a high priced market; don't try tipping my recommended minimum in an upscale bar in Manhattan.

➤**Who should be tipped.** You should tip anyone who makes or serves you a drink. Those bussing tables or restocking the bar (barbacks) get tipped out by the BTs and waitresses, so it isn't necessary to tip them, but if you've been at your table for over an hour and they've made several trips to your table they would certainly appreciate it. Occasionally barbacks, unless they are prohibited from this by management, will make drinks when the BT is slammed. Under these circumstances, they should be tipped just like a BT.

Some people seem to think that they have to tip waitresses who are transporting drinks, but that they don't need to tip BTs because they're just standing there. These are the jokers who typically sit in the waitress's area but go up to the bar for their drinks. These people are getting on the bad side of both the waitress, whose table space they're taking up, and the BT whose time they're wasting. Bottom line: if you're drinking in a bar you should be tipping someone.

While I'm on the subject, I'd like to point out that, ideally, if you're sitting in the waitress' area, you should be tipping her, whether you are getting your drinks from her or directly from the BT. You are, by sitting in her area, taking up the limited space she has in which to make her nightly income. When you get up to go, you should leave her something for the use of her space.

►Who should tip. Anyone who drinks in a bar: friends of the owner (friends of the owner who don't tip are despised by BTs), friends of the bartender's (then she'll probably buy you a drink), persons who receive a free drink (even for their birthday), women (no matter how pretty), men (no matter how macho), persons who feel they work harder for their money than BTs (then what are you doing wasting it on booze in a bar, Gomer?) and persons who can't afford to tip (then you can't afford to drink in a bar).

►When. My advice is to tip after each round of drinks. Some people feel that they should tip in one big chunk when they are ready to go. If you're a regular and the BT knows you, this is okay. But if the BT isn't familiar with you, you should tip after every round, otherwise the BT will assume you're a stiff, and you'll find it increasingly difficult to get a drink. As stated above, BTs are constantly assessing each customer's tipping habits. All they have to go on is the tips they see falling on the bar. If they see nothing, they have to assume there is no tip.

Another mistake is to leave a large pile of money on the bar and pay for your drinks from this pile. This gives the BT no indication of what sort of a tipper you are. It also gives other bar patrons the opportunity to rob you. People will steal your money if you leave it lying on the bar.

►With What. Bills or quarters. You should avoid using pennies, nickels or dimes for any transaction in a bar. Bars don't use these smaller coins; they just get in the way. While I personally have little problem with change if it isn't excessive, some BTs become very annoyed by its use. This is especially true when the entire tip consists of a variety of these coins which adds up to less than a 10% tip. It isn't unheard of for BTs to throw chump change over the bar at customers who leave such insults.

Tipping

➤Will the BT notice I've left a tip when the bar is slammed?
Yes, usually. BT's tend to pay attention to who's tipping and who isn't, even when the bar is slammed, but occasionally they do lose track. If you want to get credit for your tip, then it behooves you to make your tips as obvious as possible. Try to leave your tip while the BT is still facing you. This can be difficult if the BT is slammed and has moved on to the next customer before you can accomplish this. If you've just made a trip to the bar for a drink and have an empty glass or bottle in your hand, leave your tip under it. When the BT returns to bus your glass, the tip will be there, and the glass can help jog the BT's memory as to who left the tip, particularly if you're drinking the same drink each round. This will also prevent your tip from getting knocked off the bar or mixed up with someone else's tip or change. By far the best way to insure that the BT is aware of your tip is to wave off the change, or to simply walk away without collecting it when the BT returns from the register. Of course, this doesn't work if you're paying with a bill that's far larger than your payment.

➤When a tip is implied in your payment. If your payment is in the form of two or more bills and one or more of them is left unbroken by the exchange the BT will interpret the remainder as a tip. For instance, your order comes to $4.25. If you give the BT $5, you will get seventy-five-cents in change. If you give the BT $6, you will get nothing in change. Why? Because there's no reason to add the extra dollar to your payment unless it's a tip; the five covers the bill. If you are involved in the above transaction and want to give the BT a one-dollar tip, then give her $5 to cover your order and when you receive the seventy-five cents change, pick it up and put the dollar in its place.

The only time this rule doesn't hold is when the

extra amount is far greater than a good tip. For instance, your order comes to $10 and all you have is a ten and a five, so you give the BT both bills. Most BT's will recognize that you want five singles so that you can leave a proper tip, because a 50% tip is out of the norm. My advice, however, is to ask for singles to avoid any possible confusion.

➤**When the size of an expected tip is inferred by your change.** Your order comes to $4.50, you pay with a ten and get five ones and two quarters in change. This is a hint: the BT is saying that 50 cents isn't going to cut it as a tip. You don't have to leave more, but if you don't, your next round may take awhile.

➤**Free drinks.** You should always tip for a free drink, at least as much as you would have tipped if you had paid for the drink; ideally, you should tip more.

➤**Restaurant bars.** When having a drink at a bar in a restaurant always leave a tip at the bar before being seated at your table, otherwise, the server will end up pocketing 85-90 percent of the tip intended for the BT.

➤**When it's unnecessary to tip.** Cigarettes, water and matches, when provided to you by the BT, don't require a tip. However, if you're drinking a lot of water, asking for one glass after another, you should consider tipping 50 cents to avoid annoying the BT.

➤**Nursing drinks.** Even if you tip well and otherwise behave yourself you can run afoul of your BT if you sit there and nurse one drink all night long. This is especially true on a busy night. As I've mentioned elsewhere, the BT only has so much time to make his living each night. He also has only so much space. If you're taking up valuable space at the bar but not buying more

Tipping

than one drink every hour or so the BT will become increasingly annoyed by your presents.

►**What tips won't get you.** A tip won't buy you friendship or get you a date with a BT, it won't necessarily get you extra alcohol or free drinks, and it doesn't give you the right to act like a fool. A BT may float you a drink if you're a good tipper, but don't expect it. You can tip 100%, but if you're arrogant, obnoxious, or annoying, you won't get anything extra, and if you push it too far, you'll be cut off and/or bounced. Tipping insures prompt service and will usually make your interactions with the BT more pleasant. Everything else must be earned.

►**One additional reason to tip.** Since bars are social meeting places and they are presided over by the BT it behooves you to be on the good side of this person. A BT can help or hinder your social interactions while in his domain.

For instance, it won't facilitate your efforts to impress the woman sitting next to you if the BT calls attention to your cheapness.

Or, if you are that woman, and you have been stiffing the BT, he isn't likely to intercede when the cheapskate starts to bore you with stories about how fast he drives his Corvette.

Besides this, in most bars you will encounter regulars, and if regulars see you stiffing the BT, believe me, your stock will drop.

GUZZEL & BURP

BRAND BEER

An old world tradition, brewed for American taste!

IS IT TRULY THE NECTAR OF THE GODS, OR JUST THE URINE OF YEAST? YOU DECIDE.

ANSWER: BOTH ARE CORRECT. YEAST ARE THE GODS!

JUST GUZZLE IT, THEN BURP; IT'S THAT EASY!

ALSO: TRY OUR DARK BEER: GUZZEL & BELCH OR OUR ALE: GUZZEL AND PISS ON YOURSELF

PART 2

the Product

Sit in a bar long enough and you will hear numerous beliefs concerning the attributes of alcohol. They run the gamut from aesthetics to health to the types of highs you get from different beverages. I'm no authority and can make no claims as to the validity of any of my beliefs, but I am entitled to my opinion. With that disclaimer firmly established, what follows is a brief list of my opinions.

➤**Taste.** Sometimes you will have a drink and it won't taste the way you expect it to taste. Perhaps it's a favorite beverage you've had many times before, but this time it doesn't taste quite right.

Alcohol

You suspect the BT has, dishonestly, slipped you well booze in place of the more expensive call liquor you ordered. Sometimes this is the case, but it's far more likely that one of the following has happened:

1. You've been drinking or eating something else before ordering the current drink, and it's affecting your sense of taste or you're coming down with a cold and it's affecting your sense of taste.

2. The BT has made a mistake and served you the wrong booze. Sometimes this is because the BT has misunderstood you, or has gotten confused (BTs often have more than one thing on their minds). Sometimes, particularly in the case of well booze, the bottles in the speed well have inadvertently been switched, and the BT has poured the wrong booze. The bottles in the well are always kept in the same order so the BT doesn't have to look each time he reaches for one. If the bottles become mixed up it's as if the keys on your keyboard were rearranged.

3. Your drink has been contaminated; in the case of vodka martinis it doesn't take much. If the BT hasn't bothered to rinse out his mixing vessel the residue from the last drink could alter the taste of your martini. Or, if he has recently opened a new bottle of vodka and put a pour spout on it that hasn't been rinsed out, then whatever booze that spout was previously on will contaminate the taste of your drink.

➤**Appearances.** Sometimes a drink will look different than you expect it to look. This can be caused by the lighting in the bar or by the type of glassware used by the bar.

➤**No-hangover booze.** There is no such thing. It's an advertising ploy used by certain vodka makers and is based on a partial truth. It has been found that trace substances in the amber-colored liquors can cause health problems over the long run, and in the short run can add to your hangover misery. When vodka makers claim that they've removed all the impurities, rendering their product hang-over-free, what they fail to mention is that alcohol itself is an "impurity" as far as your body is concerned, and it makes up 40% of their product. The only sure way to avoid a hangover is abstinence. Drink enough of any alcoholic beverage and you will get a hangover.

➤**Drinking water to avoid a hangover.** This is more likely to be true than the above. Alcohol is a diuretic; it causes you to urinate. Hangovers are due, in part, to dehydration. The theory is to counteract this by taking in large quantities of water. It probably also helps by cutting down on the amount of alcohol you drink during the course of an evening, because it takes time to drink water that might otherwise be spent drinking alcohol, and when you're through, you probably don't feel like drinking anything for a while.

➤**Drinking up the ladder.** There's a popular belief that you will avoid getting sick if you drink up, rather than down, the ladder. What this means is that if you've been drinking wine and want to change beverages, you should choose distilled spirits, not beer, for your next drink. I don't know if this works, but I see no reason it should.

If drinking causes you to vomit, it's usually because you've simply, drunk too much. Personally, I break this rule every time I eat out in a restaurant; I start with a martini before

Alcohol

dinner, drink wine with my dinner, have a shot of scotch or bourbon after dinner, and later, after my dinner has settled, I switch to my favorite drink—beer. I have never vomited due to drinking like this.

➤**Drinking on an empty stomach.** The reason people warn you against this is because food in your stomach slows the absorption rate of alcohol into your blood stream. The alcohol gets into your blood stream much more quickly on an empty stomach, and you become drunk faster.

➤**Drinking beer on a full stomach.** From personal experience I can attest that this isn't a good idea. The reason why is that beer, when thrown on top of a large meal, particularly one containing a lot of carbohydrates, causes the contents of the stomach to swell. In extreme cases, though not suffering from nausea, people have been known to voluntarily visit the vomitorium just to relieve the pressure.

➤**Mixing alcoholic beverages causes hangovers and/or makes you sick.** There could be something to this, but I doubt it. What's really going on here is amateur drinking. If you watch experienced drinkers, they drink the same thing all night at a very regular rate. They drink the same thing every night they go out. In this way they gauge how drunk they are getting. Experienced drinkers know how drunk they should be at any given point in the evening. If they feel they're getting ahead of themselves, they back off for a while. Offer them something different than what they've been drinking and they will tell you that they "don't change horses midstream."

Amateurs jump from one thing to the next, sipping one, shooting another, guzzling the one after that. Mid-drink their friend orders a round of shooters and they do them at once and go back to what they were drinking when the shooter was proffered. First, it's a cosmopolitan, then a shot of Jagermeister, then a Long Island Iced Tea sounds like a good idea. These people are hammered before they know what hit them. That night they throw up, the next morning they awake with a horrible hangover and blame it all on the fact that they were mixing their drinks. It wasn't the mixture, it was the quantity and the rate.

►**Hair of the dog.** A time-honored hangover cure. The expression stems from a belief in folk medicine which dates back to before the Romans. This form of healthcare holds that if something ails you you need to ingest a minute quantity of the agent suspected of causing your disease. In full form the expression is, "A hair of the dog that bit you," apparently referring to a guard against rabies; ingest a hair of the dog that bit you, and you will avoid getting rabies. Drinkers using this excuse for a morning drink are entering a vicious circle. A drink will definitely "cure" a hangover, but it does so by getting you drunk again. When it wears off, you will have a hangover again and need another curative.

►**People who don't get hangovers.** Anyone who drinks enough to get drunk will get a hangover. Perhaps not every time, but more often than not. People who drink but claim never to get hangovers are, most likely, chronic alcoholics who drink to the same degree of drunkenness everyday. Every morning they wake up feeling the same so they say they don't get hangovers. If you woke up, feeling the way they feel when they wake up, you'd call it a hangover.

►**Different highs from different beverages.** I have personally

Alcohol

never noticed this to be the case, but many people claim to get a different high from tequila than they do from beer than they do from vodka. I do notice that I get drunker and do stupider things if I drink distilled spirits along with my beer, rather than just sticking to beer, and I notice heavier-bodied beers make me feel more relaxed than light-bodied ones, but it all seems to be more or less the same feeling: drunkenness. I have drunk tequila and Jagermeister and never felt anything other than drunk. I've even drunk the illegal absinthe and Risea (a Mexican liquor I've surely misspelled) and never felt anything but drunk. On the other hand, when I've smoked pot or opium, taken LSD or snorted cocaine, I've felt quite a bit different. Maybe I'm just insensitive.

➤**Nonalcoholic beer.** Bars carry this product primarily for alcoholics who are on the wagon or who have quit indefinitely, but whose lives still revolve around bars. People who don't have a drinking problem will drink real beer if that's what they want to taste. People who have never been drinkers have no reason to want something that tastes vaguely like beer; they will order Coke, water or juice. Two of the exceptions to this rule are: pregnant women or others who must avoid alcohol for medical reasons, and designated drivers.

➤**The wagon.** One sure sign that a person is an alcoholic is if they "go on the wagon," particularly if they do it at some regular time during the year. For most people this period falls in January, right after the holidays; the heaviest drinking period of the year. As for myself, I go on the wagon during the holidays; the day before Thanksgiving until New Year's.

Alcohol

➤**Hiccups.** The BT's cure for the hiccups is lime and bitters. Put a lime wedge in a rocks glass and soak it with four or five dashes of bitters. The hiccup sufferer then shoots the whole business into their mouth, chews it up and swallows it. This cures the hiccups about half of the time.

➤**Sleep.** Alcohol can have a damaging effect upon your sleep patterns. If you don't believe this now, then someday you will. You may already have experienced sleep deprivation and not known it because you attributed your exhaustion, after sleeping for a longer than normal period, to a hangover. What has happened is that you did not really sleep much at all, you were passed out and never got into a R. E. M. sleep state.

The second type of sleep deprivation is insomnia. You may experience it either upon going to bed drunk and finding it impossible to fall asleep, or after passing out for four or five hours and then waking up in a wired state, unable to fall back to sleep even though you are exhausted. I've been told by many people (none of them doctors) that this is due to the sugars in alcoholic beverages. Alcohol is sugar, or other carbohydrates, converted by the action of yeast. The yeast organisms eat sugar, then excrete alcohol; this process is called *fermentation* (that's right, alcohol is the urine of yeast!). I guess the idea is that when the drug, alcohol, wears off, the excess energy generated by the digestion of the alcohol and/or the residual sugars in incompletely fermented beverages, causes you to become wired. There could be something to this, but I suspect it's a little more complex than that.

➤**Sex.** Much the same as sleep, you will eventually have problems in this area even if up until now you've noticed no effect or even had an enhancement of sexual abilities. It will affect different people at different ages, but eventually alcohol takes its toll. Only men will be directly affected, but it certainly can't be a source of joy to a woman whose sex partner is unable to perform after imbibing too much.

However, alcohol, on average, takes a greater toll on a woman's appearance than on a man's. So, though a woman who regularly drinks too much may still be able to perform sexually, she will find it increasingly difficult to find acceptable partners.

►**Eating/weight effects.** Alcohol is the only drug that has food value. An ounce of beer has about 13 calories. An ounce of wine has about 20 calories. And an ounce of distilled spirits has about 53 calories. If your weekly diet stays the same but you add to it several drinks, then it's possible to add several hundred calories to your diet and a weight gain could result. However, since alcohol contains calories, the effect of one or more drinks is often to suppress your appetite. If the calories you take, in the form of alcohol, are offset by an equal number of calories lost by not eating, you may experience no weight gain, and if you expend extra calories due to supplementary activities caused by drinking, dancing, for instance, then you could actually lose weight. Conversely, if drinking causes you to become more sedentary you may gain weight even though you are taking in the same number of calories.

If drinking becomes a problem and calories from alcohol supplant much of your caloric intake from other sources, then you will not only lose weight but your body will begin to deteriorate, since the calories represented by alcohol are devoid of nutritional value and because alcohol is a poison when taken in sufficient quantities. The fact that alcohol is a diuretic is another

Alcohol

problem. Many alcoholics suffer from dehydration, which increases weight loss and has serious health consequences.

➤**Health problems.** In addition to those mentioned above, there is a host of health problems related to alcohol. As I have no medical training, I can only point out a few of the obvious ones. I'm sure a doctor could add to this list:

➤**Cirrhosis of the liver.**

➤**Increased risk of cancer.**

➤**Heart problems.**

➤**General lowering of personal hygiene standards leading to other health problems.**

➤**Cuts, bruises, broken bones, loss of teeth.**

➤**The D.t.'s. / Mental disorientation.**

➤**Depression.**

➤**Accidental death** due to falls, traffic accidents, boating accidents, house fires, alcohol poisoning, extreme dissipation or exposure to the elements.

➤**Loss of productivity.** You will miss more work, clean your house less, make payments of bills in a less timely fashion, pay less attention to your personal appearance, have less money to spend on other interests in your life, have less other interests in your life, fail in your social relationships more often, spend more time in jail and/or court, be more likely to have your driver's license suspended or revoked, pay more for car insurance, lose more jobs, spend more on doctor bills and be more likely to default on bank loans if you allow alcohol to run your life.

For more graphic information on this subject you need look no further than city streets. Huddled there you will find legions of people who went too far in their love for alcohol.

And now for the good news...

➤**Health benefits.** A few drinks a day can have a beneficial effect on your health. Lower blood pressure and lower stress levels are two that come to mind. There is some evidence that alcohol in moderation can lower cholesterol levels. Whatever the claims or evidence the key is *moderation*, which means one to three drinks per day. More than that and the benefits are outweighed by the negative effects.

➤**Cure for the common cold.** Some people feel that a shot of whiskey, perhaps mixed with hot water and a little sugar, is a way to deal with a cold. While it will make you feel better it has no effect on your cold other than to lower your body's defenses to the organism which is causing your problems. The best thing you can do when you come down with a cold is to lay off the sauce.

➤**Recreation.** While more than three drinks can be harmful to a degree there is such a thing as being too health-conscious. Life is meant to be enjoyed, and a long, dull life isn't something I feel is worth pursuing. Occasionally, getting drunk can be worth the increased health risk just because it's fun. Climbing mountains, skiing, travel and sex can be health threats too, but people choose to indulge in these activities because they weigh the health threat against the amount of enjoyment derived. The same can be said for occasionally over-indulging in your favorite beverage.

➤**Social activities.** Most interaction can be enhanced and revved up by the introduction of alcohol. People become more animated under the influence of alcohol, and this can add excitement to any social situation. Dancing is more fun if you're a bit looped, as are long conversations in a bar with friends, acquaintances and strangers. Parties are fueled by

Alcohol

alcohol, and I have noticed over the years that when the alcohol runs out, especially alcohol in the form of beer, the party dies.

➤**Food.** One of the reasons alcohol is so prominent in our western culture is that it goes so well with food and is in fact a part of a good diet. A martini before dinner builds anticipation for the coming meal. Wine with dinner enhances the flavor of the food. An after-dinner drink such as bourbon, scotch or brandy aids in digestion and is very relaxing. The only other drugs that play a part in a good meal are tobacco and coffee, but their roles are minor in comparison. Oh yeah, and pot, which is not so much an enhancement to a good meal as it is an agent used to make any food product seem appealing in large amounts.

➤**Restorative powers.** There's nothing like a beer after work. It relaxes you as it quenches your thirst, soothes aching muscles and brightens your outlook on life.

➤**Pain killer.** Whether it's an aching back or an aching heart, alcohol can help. While I wouldn't recommend it for sufferers of mental illness or long term problems, its ability to brighten your outlook on life in the short term can help you to overcome the minor aches, pains and depressions of life.

➤**Conversation.** Sitting, talking, and drinking beer is one of my favorite pastimes. One of the truly positive experiences associated with alcohol is its effect on conversation. If several people are sitting down to converse it's amazing to watch the effects of alcohol on the conversation. What would otherwise be a minor disagreement becomes a full-fledged argument. A subject, which had seemed dull,

Alcohol

now commands enthusiastic attention. What began as a boring evening has turned into an exciting one, thanks to the old demon alcohol.

➤**Ideas.** Many good ideas come with the help of a little alcohol, sometimes while talking with someone, other times while just sitting quietly drinking in a bar. The relaxing and uninhibiting effects of this drug allows for ideas that would otherwise be repressed to float gently to the surface.

➤**Bonding.** People who drink together form bonds more readily. This is because when people drink they exhibit parts of their personalities that they otherwise might hide. If you know them in their sober state, this additional information about them can help to cement a relationship. If it's the only way you encounter them then the relationship won't be a very sound one.

➤**Joint projects.** Just as with personal relationships, projects can benefit by occasional meetings in bars. People loosen up; alcohol brings them together and levels the social strata. The boss gets drunk when she drinks, just like everybody else. An underling feels free to voice doubts about some aspect of the project. People become jovial, and bonds among team members are strengthened. This goes for groups of artists as well as for groups of real estate agents.

➤**Meeting people.** Because alcohol lowers inhibitions, it's great for meeting people. Sitting in a bar you are more likely to strike up a conversation with a stranger, and the stranger is more likely to respond positively when you do. Shy people have newfound social skills and the already socially adept are like kids in a candy store, not knowing where to turn next for a new conversation with a new face.

➤*Amour.* If you're looking for physically intimate contact, alcohol is a proven catalyst. It's no guarantee, but your chances improve when alcohol enters the picture. Someone who was mildly attractive to you earlier in the evening may begin to look much better after a few drinks. As a friend of mine in the army once bragged, "I've never been to bed with an ugly woman, but I've woken up with dozens of them; I drink them pretty." Of course, this works for women as well.

The danger here, as we all know, is waking up with someone you'd rather not wake up with. It can be an awkward moment upon awakening to find yourself in a strange bed in a strange part of town with the sun streaming through the window and no shades in your pocket. This can be more than embarrassing or humiliating, it can be dangerous. The best advice is not to get so drunk that you make bad decisions. Of course, advice is much easier to give than to receive.

PART 3

the
**Human
Element**

One thing every BT knows is that you must remain in charge of the bar at all times. If you let an unruly, arrogant, violent or drunken person take charge for even a moment, you're asking for trouble. If you let it happen on a regular basis, you're out of a job. This is one of the hardest parts of bartending; any fool can pour gin into a glass and hand it to a drunk. It takes a little more intelligence to keep a drunk happy while you're telling him he's had too much and you won't serve him anymore.

For this reason BTs will let you know when you've stepped over the line. All BTs realize that

Who's In Charge Here?

in a bar people are using a powerful drug, alcohol, and what would be considered aberrant behavior elsewhere is to be expected. To what degree it is tolerated depends on the parameters of the particular bar and BT you're dealing with. However, there are some guidelines that obtain in pretty much every bar:

➤**Bringing your own drinks into/out of a bar.** Unless you're in New Orleans, don't do this. BTs frown on patrons bringing their own drinks into their bar because they're in the business of selling booze. They frown on patrons who take drinks out of their bar because it is illegal.

Consequently, persons attempting to leave with a drink will usually be prevented from doing so. Persons attempting to enter with an open container will be told to leave it outside. Open containers found in the bar are viewed as a form of theft, so they are confiscated and poured out. The exception to this is people who bring in their own bottle of wine or champagne and ask the BT's permission to do so. This is usually allowed, with a corkage fee charged for each bottle. If it's a large party with a single bottle, the BT will often figure it's worth the goodwill to waive the corkage fee as they will polish off the bottle quickly, then start buying their drinks from the bar.

The idea is that a bar is a place of business and BTs are working to make a living. You wouldn't take a picnic lunch into a restaurant; don't bring your own drinks into a bar.

➤**Excessive drinking.** There is a misconception among some people that BTs like drunks. Nothing could be further from the truth. BTs hate drunks. They're what make the job a pain in the ass at times. People who order strange concoctions made from several liquors then shoot them down in between guzzling large quantities of more prosaic beverages in a silly attempt to get as drunk as possible in the shortest amount of time don't impress BTs, except with the fact that they're idiots and probably inexperienced drinkers.

 Don't get me wrong, bars are places that sell alcohol, so people are going to get drunk—but how drunk? That depends on the bar, the BT, and the situation. But there is a point at which a customer becomes too drunk to be served. Beyond this point the customer will become a potential danger to all involved. At the very least he will become a source of annoyance to those around him. When this point is reached, there's no choice but to cut him off.

►**Not enough booze.** Customers will occasionally return a drink because there isn't enough booze in it. These are usually people who are drinking highballs. Sometimes it's people who are drinking talls! It's almost always people who have been drinking a lot. I never give these jokers extra booze, I simply explain to them how they should order in the future if they want to taste the booze—with a splash (of mixer).

►**Buying friends drinks when they don't want and/or need one.** Often customers will offer to buy a friend a drink. This is part of drinking in a bar. However, BTs can be expected to refuse this request in either of two scenarios: the friend in question is too drunk, or the friend in question declines the offer. Occasionally the customer offering to buy the drink will then demand that the BT serve the drink anyway. The customer is wrong. BTs, as elsewhere noted, must remain in

Who's In Charge Here?

charge of the situation. The BT is also in a better position to judge the situation. If the friend of the customer feels he or she is too drunk for another drink then it's in the BT's best interest not to serve the drink. The same is true if the friend is obviously too drunk to handle another drink. Customers who become belligerent due to the BT's refusal to serve their friend an additional drink under these circumstances are asking to be cut off themselves.

➤**Buying drinks for a person who has been cut off.** This is similar to the situation noted above. The way it usually transpires is a customer will be cut off at the bar for any of several reasons. After a brief argument with the BT, the customer wanders away. A moment later, another customer comes to the bar and orders the same drink that the first customer was denied. To the BT it is obvious what's going on: he's being played for a chump.

➤**Doubles, lining up drinks.** I prefer not to serve doubles or to line up drinks because it's harder to control how drunk the customer is becoming. If it's a person I'm familiar with, I don't mind, because I know their drinking habits. If it's a large person, I'm not concerned, because they can absorb a lot of booze. But I watch those customers unknown to me and of average size who order doubles or line up drinks. At the first sign that they're going over the deep end I cut them off.

Something to keep in mind is you don't get a bulk discount on booze; a double costs twice as much as a single. The only thing you save when you order doubles is time.

➤**Cutting off drunks.** This is a sticky wicket. Customers

are not always amenable to this and may become indignant and/or violent. My course of action, unless I'm dealing with an idiot, is to offer the customer something else, such as water or coffee, which helps to soften the blow of being turned down, which can be embarrassing to the customer if he still possesses the clarity of thought to be embarrassed.

Even more problematic is that it's not always obvious that a customer is drunk. Many drunks are able to sober up long enough to order a drink. Often I've served a seemingly sober person only to see him staggering around moments later. This usually happens with a customer who has just arrived from another bar where he has gotten tanked up and possibly been ejected for drunkenness.

These are usually customers I'm not familiar with. I know the tells of the regulars. Strangers are not so easy. I often must serve them one drink before I can tell if they've had too much. BTs help each other out by notifying each other when they realize they've served a drunk or when they see a customer they've had trouble with in the past enter the bar.

In other cases it's much easier to tell. One thing that's a dead giveaway is a customer with her head on the bar. This is bad. It not only looks bad to have people passed out on the bar, but it becomes a safety problem as well. It also presents a dilemma if it's near the end of the night, because you have to get rid of the customer before closing but your options for doing so are few. No cab driver wants to pick up a comatose person because then the person becomes his problem. You can't just throw them out on the street for both ethical and legal reasons. The usual method of dealing with customers whose heads are on the bar is to rouse them, and once aroused to get them moving toward the door as soon as possible.

Who's In Charge Here?

Other obvious signs that a customer has had too much are falling off of a barstool and spilling drinks. If a customer falls off his barstool, I cut him off, unless there's some reason other than drunkenness for the fall. If a customer spills his drink, I usually replace it if they don't seem drunk. If they spill it a second time, I assume that they're just good at covering their drunkenness, and I cut them off.

Then there are those people whom anyone can tell are drunk: they stagger in off the street, they wander around the bar talking loudly, annoying people, bumping into patrons, furniture, and generally making a nuisance of themselves. These people don't belong in a bar.

In these cases, and the ones I haven't mentioned, you often find that the customer who's been cut off will want to argue the point and try to convince you that you're mistaken. My rule of thumb here is that once I've made the decision to cut someone off I don't go back on it. My stock response to such arguments is "I do make mistakes and if you feel I'm wrong you're welcome to get a second opinion at some other bar from some other bartender."

►**Don't treat the BT as a servant.** BTs are members of the service industry. They make your drinks and serve them to you. They wipe up your spills, empty your ashtrays and perform other tasks so that you can enjoy a few drinks with your friends. However, if you want to get on the bad side of a BT, the quickest way to do so is to treat her as a servant. A couple of examples of this sort of behavior would be snapping your fingers and/or yelling "Hey!" to get her attention or, just as bad, banging an empty glass on the bar. These examples pale when compared with such verbal treats as "If you want my business you should learn how to serve me."

▶**NEVER WALK BEHIND THE BAR.** Not even one step.

▶**Last call.** When last call is sounded, that's the time to order your last drink, not ten minutes later. If you wait ten minutes you probably won't get a drink. If you do order at last call make sure you can drink it in the time remaining, keeping in mind that most bars go by bar time, which is anywhere from ten to twenty minutes ahead of real time. When the time comes to give up your drink, give it up.

Some people you see in bars just seem to fit in. Their manner is very comfortable, they're always able to get a drink. They encounter few if any problems, and they get along well with the BT and the other customers, even if they're not regulars.

Other people are always in the way of bar staff and other customers. They have trouble getting served and are often in an argument over some perceived transgression.

The difference between the two groups described above is that the first group knows the unwritten etiquette of bars, the second group does not. What follows is my effort to change that unwritten status, and while not complete, it is a start.

►**Getting the BT's attention**. This usually isn't a problem when business is slow, but it can be when the bar is slammed. The wait probably isn't as long as you think, time being relative, but when you want a drink, ten minutes can seem excessive. To help you cut down on this wait time you must first see things from the BT's perspective.

A BT will try to serve customers in roughly the order they come to the bar. Make eye contact. This will put you on the BT's mental waiting list. Have your money out and visible. This tells the BT that, at the very least, you are ready to pay and won't slow things down with a bill-by-bill inventory of your wallet, pocket or purse. Beyond that, it's been my experience that customers who have their money out have their order ready, and that's what a busy BT wants: customers who know what they want and have their money at the ready. However, don't make the mistake of waving bills in the air—BTs hate this. Instead, take a bill in your hand and rest that hand on the bar, holding the bill so that it's visible. Any BT who sees this will know it means that you're ready to order.

►**Getting served.** BTs are human and as such will be attracted to certain customers for a variety of reasons that have nothing to do with either fairness or a first-come-first-served policy; they are taller, so they stand out; they are attractive members of the opposite sex, so they stand out; they are attractive members of the same sex, so they stand out; they are friends or regulars, so the BT recognizes them; they are customers who have recently been served and left a

Bar Etiquette

large tip, etc. If you don't fall into any of these categories you can, by standing in close proximity to persons who do, increase your chances of being served.

For instance, you're in a very busy bar and there's a tall, attractive female waiting to get a drink. If you stand next to her you stand a good chance of being the one served right after her simply because when the BT has completed the transaction with her, you will be standing right there. You must follow the other rules, however: make eye contact and have your money visible. Be sure that when the BT returns to complete the transaction with her that you're not chatting with friends or looking around the room, because you can lose this slight advantage in an instant if the BT returns, gives her her change, looks to you and finds that you're otherwise engaged. By the time you look up the BT has moved on to the next customer, the one who's been paying attention.

Related to the above is the phenomenon of "hot-spots" and "cold-spots." When a bar is slammed hot-spots will develop. What is happening is the BT, when returning to give the current customer change will immediately be confronted by the next customer who is standing nearby. When returning with that customer's change there will be another customer standing there waiting for service, etc. Similarly, there will be cold-spots at the bar that the BT can't get to because she is caught in a hot-spot. When this happens you can try to move into the hot-spot, but this area is often too crowded to get to. A better bet is to be patient; she's aware that you're there and will get to you as soon as she gets a chance. "Hot spots" are broken when a customer pays with an amount that doesn't require change.

A contraindicated method of getting the BT's attention, that some customers seem to prefer, is to yell, "Bartender!, Bartender!" repeatedly while waving their arms frantically. While this method will get you noticed, it won't necessarily get you a drink, as it can be very annoying to have someone yelling at you in this manner when you're slammed. BTs will often neglect such customers out of revenge. It's also been my experience that customers who act in this manner usually don't have an order ready, and when you do offer to serve them will turn to their friends to ask what everybody wants.

Another thing that can slow down your service is to seat yourself at the bar where someone has just vacated and left behind several glasses. Scanning the bar the subliminal image the BT gets is one of a customer with a drink. This is especially true when the BT is slammed. The thing to do is to push the glasses into a group and toward the BT's side of the bar, not so far that they might fall over the edge, but far enough so that the BT will get the image of "dead ones" on the bar.

All said, your best bet is patience. No BT is going to let a customer get away from the bar without a drink if it can be helped. There are times when a bar is hit with an unexpected volume of business and getting a drink becomes a problem. This situation is most often the fault of your fellow customers rather than the bar staff, as customers who don't know what they're doing slow the whole process down.

On the other hand, if you've been stiffing the BT earlier in the evening, the bar has recently become slammed, and you now find it difficult to get a drink, if it seems that the BT keeps passing you by to serve customers that haven't been waiting as long as you have, it's time to go, pal, you're done in this bar.

Bar Etiquette

►**Conversation with a BT.** People like to talk to BTs and BTs like to talk to customers. It's also true that BTs are there to make a living and other customers want to get a drink. These last two facts take precedence over the first two. If you're in a conversation with a BT, be ready to hold that thought. Use common sense: if the bar is busy, don't try to involve the BT in long-winded stories or jokes. If the BT suddenly begs off in the middle of your story and moves down the bar, don't take it personally.

A BT's work week is generally much shorter than that of other professions. That's one of the draws of the job, that you can support yourself on a 25-30 hour work week. The other side of the coin is that you can't afford to slack off even for a minute when the business is there. During a six-hour shift a BT may make most of his money during the two or three hours when the bar is at its busiest. During that period you've got to be moving at top efficiency or it will cost you money.

It's not just the money it costs you personally, because you're often working with another BT and pooling tips. One way to get on the bad side of your fellow BTs is to stand chatting while they do all the work. Then there are your customers. They are impatient when you're slammed, but if you're standing there jackin' yer jaws and they can't get a drink, they take it personally.

Friends and lovers is another sticky subject for BTs when they're on duty. If a good friend is sitting at your bar, you want to talk to him but you sometimes can't, for the reasons stated above. Friends and lovers of those in the bar trade have to understand that. Those who need constant attention would

the HEARTBREAK of HAT HAIR

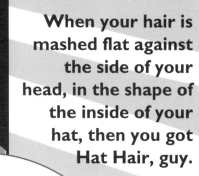

GUY WITH HAT

When your hair is mashed flat against the side of your head, in the shape of the inside of your hat, then you got Hat Hair, guy.

GUY WITH HAT HAIR

Bar Etiquette

do best not to visit their BT pals while they're on duty, or at least avoid visiting during peak hours.

►**Don't block the service station.** At a busy bar the most open spot is the service station. It's okay to order here so long as you stay alert to the location of the server. When the server approaches you should make way immediately. Servers are often carrying trays heavy with bussed glassware when they approach the service station, and they want to put it down as quickly as possible. They also are trying to make a living, and the quicker they can give their order to the BT and get their order filled, the quicker they can deliver their orders and come back for another.

If you do order from the service station, get away from it as soon as you receive your drinks. For some reason people like to hover around this area, which blocks the path of the server and other customers. Don't do this.

►**Don't crowd the flap.** This is the part of the bar that lifts up. It can be lowered to extend the bar but usually it's left up because it's the only way out from behind the bar. There are many reasons BTs need to come out from behind the bar: restocking, getting ice, using the restroom, dealing with problems of various sorts both natural and man-made. When the BT isn't using this exit, the barback is. If you're standing there, you're in the way, you're hair in the drain, move it, pal. Don't crowd the flap.

►**Don't treat the garnish tray as a salad bar.** People often like to pluck olives or cherries from the garnish tray. If they ask first I always say yes; it would be petty to deny them such an insignificant item. However, if someone begins grazing on my olives, I'm forced to say something. I have to spear those olives in advance to save time. If I run low, I have to stop and spear some more. This costs me time that could be used to make drinks, which in turn costs me money.

There's also the factor of cleanliness. My hands are usually quite clean while I'm bartending because I'm always washing glasses in between making drinks. The same can't be said for customer's hands, and other customers don't necessarily like to see a lot of different hands on the garnish that may eventually end up in their drinks. For these reasons, it's best to keep this behavior to a minimum.

➤**Bar kibble.** If you need a snack a better move would be to ask the BT if she has any bar snacks: peanuts, pretzels, etc.

➤**Leaving drinks unattended.** If you must get up and leave your drink unattended, the accepted signal that you plan to return is to put a serviette (napkin) on top of it. The reason for this is that part of a BT's work includes busing drinks and making space for the next customer. If the BT comes to an unattended drink, especially one that is more than half empty, the normal response is to remove it from the bar, wipe the area with a bar rag and ready the space for the next customer. Customers often lose drinks and/or their seat at the bar this way and sometimes become annoyed with the BT, who has simply done what comes naturally. It's the customer's responsibility to signal the BT, either verbally or with a serviette, that the drink is still in play. This is especially important in bars where no smoking laws are being enforced as there are many people compelled to leave their drinks at the bar while they go outside for a smoke.

Another mistake customers make that causes them to lose

Bar Etiquette

their drinks is to set them down on the service station, which is also the bussing station. Any drink showing up here is considered dead and is quickly bussed.

▶**Buying drinks in advance.** Sometimes a customer will offer to buy a drink for someone at the bar who has a full drink. Rather than serve the drink which will wilt before the recipient can get to it, the BT will take payment for the drink, then put a shot or rocks glass, upside-down, in front of the person for whom the drink was purchased. This is then redeemable by the recipient when they are ready for it.

▶**Shaking the BT's hand.** People often want to shake the BT's hand, usually upon arrival at or departure from the bar. This is fine but when the BT is busy it's not a good idea because, like other people, a BT only has two hands and both are in use when the bar is busy. At this time, it's best to use a visual or verbal form of greeting. Also, remember that a BT's hand is usually wet.

▶**Being your own server/busser.** Serving yourself and your friends from the bar is fine but you should know a little something about how to do it. The most glasses you should attempt to carry at one time is three. You should carry them in a triangular configuration with both hands, like a rack of pool balls, one in the front, two in the back. Never try to carry four or more because chances are you will drop them before you get back to your table.

Occasionally, a customer will ask for a tray to carry an order back to his table. I always tell him that I don't have a tray, which is a lie. The last thing I want to see is a customer with a tray of drinks negotiating the distance back to his table; the possibility for disaster here is great.

Bussing your glassware is less of a problem and is appreciated by the BT, particularly if he's slammed and/or working without a busser. Just make sure that when you set them on the bar you don't put them too near the edge or stack them too high. Personally, I don't like them higher than three glasses. The reason for this is that they become unstable over that height. If they get knocked over, the glasses are likely to break. If they break in the ice well the BT is going to want to strangle you, so keep this in mind when bussing your own.

➤**Asking for a glass of ice.** This is the surest way to alert the BT that you've snuck your own bottle into the bar.

➤**Homeless people.** The homeless come under the heading of people who disrupt business. They will, if allowed, stay for hours and tie up the rest room for long periods. They have no money to spend so they will panhandle money, drinks and cigarettes. They will steal tips from the BT and belongings from the customers. They will harass customers and the bar staff. Because of this they are not welcome in bars. Some people find this insensitive. They feel the homeless should be treated like anyone else and allowed to remain in a bar if they choose. What these people fail to recognize is that the bar looks a lot different from behind the plank than it does from the floor. Customers can get up and leave when they want and have no responsibility for what happens in a bar. The BT doesn't have this luxury. Anyone who disrupts business is ejected, so in this way the homeless are treated like everyone else.

The homeless need help, none of which is available in a bar. People who feel strongly about the well-being of a homeless person and believe that a drink will help should take him to their home.

➤**Just came by to hang out.** For some reason there are

Bar Etiquette

people who mistakenly think that a bar is a public facility. They will drop by to sit and relax, or more often just to use the rest room. Here's a flash for those who believe this—it ain't so! Bars are private property. They are under no obligation to let you use their restroom or phone or anything else; in fact they often resent it.

➤**Picking up tips: BTs.** Some BT's pick up tips as soon as they hit the bar. Others wait until the customer leaves. This will vary from bar to bar, BT to BT, and situation to situation. Personally, I leave them for a while if the customer is sitting at the bar. If it's a customer that just came up to the bar for a drink and then leaves; then I pick it up immediately. Sometimes I leave the tips for awhile just because I'm busy and could better use the time it would take to pick them up. If it's a regular sitting at the bar I often leave them until she leaves or until she pushes them forward to the edge of the bar, making it clear that they are tips. This shows the regular that I know they leave good tips and I'm not concerned about it. I'm more likely to pick up tips quickly if they're from people I don't know, and especially if they are drinking a lot, because in these cases, when they run out of money they will often start buying drinks from their tip pile.

➤**Picking up tips: customers.** Unless it's money you've put on the bar, **don't ever do this.**

➤**Making change from tips on the bar.** Sometimes people need phone change and to save time they will make change out of the tips lying on the bar. I wouldn't advise doing this unless you first ask the BT.

➤**The "knock".** Some BTs will rap with their knuckles on the bar when they pick up tips. This signifies a number of things; first, it's a way to signal that the tip was received and to say "thank you." Secondly, it announces that the BT is collecting a tip, so it won't appear that the BT is picking up money on the sly. Lastly, it calls the attention of a stiff who is waiting for service, so that he or she will take notice and, hopefully, the hint. This practice is probably derived from card dealers in Las Vegas who knock on the table whenever they take the house cut or a tip.

➤**BT/customer confidentiality.** There is no such thing; anything you do or say can become part of the BT's repertoire or even an entry in a book like this one.

➤**Breaking large bills.** Customers will sometimes apologize for paying with a twenty. This is not a problem. Any bar except those that are mismanaged or in bad financial shape can break a twenty at any time. Fifties and "C" notes can be a problem if the bar has just opened, or if there has been a shift change and the drawer is new. But this ceases to be a problem within about half an hour after the beginning of the shift. After this, breaking a fifty or a "C" note is no different than breaking a twenty, because the bulk of the change will be in the form of twenties. In fact, BTs would rather you pay with a large bill rather than waste time searching your wallet for the correct change.

➤**Change.** Most BTs will put your change on the bar, not in your hand. There are two reasons for this: first, it's faster. You can slap it on the bar and immediately move on to the next piece of work. When you put it in someone's hand you have to be a little more genteel, which is slower. The other reason is that when it's slapped on the bar it's there for all to see and

Bar Etiquette

fewer disagreements over correct change result. If there is a disagreement, customers sitting nearby will have seen the change as well and can assist in settling the dispute.

➤**Short change.** Sometimes there is a disagreement as to the denomination of the bill tendered in a bar transaction. This can be problematic. The BT is usually right. After all, unless he's been drinking, he's sober, and the customer probably isn't. People can go through a lot of money quickly in a bar and may think they gave the BT a twenty when in fact they broke that twenty on their last transaction at the bar.

One method I use to cut down on disagreements is to call out the denomination of the bill as I take it. I always watch as the customer hands the bill over so I know what it is before I take it. As I'm about to put it in the till I look at it again.

However, I do occasionally make a mistake. When a customer insists he gave me a twenty, and I believe he gave me a ten, the first thing I do is to look in the till. If he's right I will find a twenty in the ten slot. If I don't find this to be the case I tell him he is wrong. If he wants to argue the point I tell him I will take his phone number and call him if my drawer is over at the end of the night. Or, if I'm not busy I will stop and count the drawer on the spot. This usually isn't possible, however, and customers won't always trust me to call if my drawer is over. On very rare occasions I have given the customer the extra ten they feel they deserve. I don't like doing this but sometimes it's the most economical solution for both the bar owner and myself—a disruption of business during a slammed shift is expensive.

➤**Aspirin.** Many bars will not dispense aspirins to customers

A word to smokers from Hugh Jardon:
Don't be a quitter!

"I'm not a quitter...I smoke constantly now!"-Hugh Jardon

Last month I quit smoking. After a few days I could smell things I hadn't smelled in years: bus fumes, dog shit, bum vomit.
I QUIT QUITTING!
So can you.

Bar Etiquette

even though they have them on hand for hungover BTs. The reason for this is that if a person has a bad reaction to the aspirin-alcohol mixture the bar could be sued for illegally dispensing a medicine. They aren't responsible if the customer buys their own aspirin, however, which is why you sometimes see little aspirin packets for sale in bars.

►**Smoking.** It is illegal to smoke in bars in the state of California. Of course that doesn't mean you can't smoke in bars, it just means you can't smoke in all bars. It can be confusing, but if you look around when you enter a bar and you see people smoking then it's okay to smoke. If you don't see people smoking then it would be a good idea to ask the BT what the bar's policy is. If she tells you, "You can smoke," then you can smoke. If she tells you, "You can't smoke here, it's illegal," then you can't smoke. If she tells you, "It's illegal to smoke in the state of California," especially if she says so in a monotone voice, then you can probably smoke.

The reason for this confusion is that while it may be illegal to smoke in bars there is no interest on the part of the police or the health department to enforce the law—they have more important things to deal with. The only way you are likely to run into trouble smoking in bars which allow smoking is if a beat cop enters the bar while a rabid anti-smoker is present. If this person approaches the cop and demands that he issues citations to the smokers in the room the cop is legally obligated to issue the citations. This being the case it would be wise to hide your cigarette when a cop enters the bar, at least until you can ascertain weather or not one of these self-appointed guardians of the public health is present. If you are issued a citation (I believe they are for $75) you may choose to go to court and deny that you were smoking. Chances are that when the judge calls for the arresting officer no one will respond—case dismissed.

On the other hand, knowing this and lighting up in a bar that doesn't allow smoking will simply set you up for harassment and probably a bouncing by the bar staff.

►**Clove cigarettes.** No one, not even other smokers, likes the smell of clove cigarettes. Clove cigarettes are also a dead give-away for an underage person, since most people outside of Indonesia who smoke them tend to be teenagers. So if you're sneaking into a bar underage, I wouldn't advise lighting up one of these unless you want to call attention to yourself.

►**Cigars.** These are the trendy way to smoke. They are acceptable in most bars where smoking is permitted, though ideally one should ask those nearby, including the BT, if they mind cigar smoke.

►**Pipes.** The smoke from pipes is so heavy that it's not a good idea, particularly if the bar is crowded.

►**Pot.** It's illegal and the bar didn't sell it to you, two very good reasons not to light up in a bar unless you want to get thrown out.

►**Drugs.** BTs generally frown on drug use in their bars, because it leads to other problems, the primary one being getting busted for running an establishment that allows the sale and use of illegal substances. Another is that persons under the influence of a variety of illegal drugs mixed with alcohol makes for customers whose behavior is unpredictable. Also, there's the fact that if someone is dealing drugs in a bar, they are competing with the BT; every dollar

Bar Etiquette

spent on an illegal drug is one less dollar they have to spend on alcohol.

➤**Ice.** American bars use a lot of ice. American drinks are filled with ice. If you're European or if you don't like ice in your drink, you must say so before the BT starts to fill your order. Keep in mind that because American drinks are based on the glass first being filled with ice, when you get yours without ice, the glass won't be filled to the usual level. If it were, the drink would be weak due a higher proportion of mixer. Ice takes up more than one-half the volume of the glass in a normal highball drink.

➤**Free drinks.** Most bars give away a certain amount of free drinks. The people who get them generally fall into one or more of the following five categories:

#1. People who work in the bar and restaurant business (*i.e.*, off-duty BTs and servers). These people will give you free drinks or food when you visit their place of business. They will also tell other people about your bar if they have a good time there, so it behooves both you and the bar owner to take care of them. Hence, free drinks for the bar and restaurant personnel.

#2. Regulars who spend a lot of money in your bar and help to create its personality. These people add to your cash drawer directly by the money they spend, and indirectly by the money they attract in the form of new customers. Hence, free drinks for the regulars.

#3. High-rollers who come in and spend a lot of money and tip big without being obnoxious about it. You'd like to see more of them, and to encourage their return. Hence, free drinks for the high-rollers.

Anyone who wears shades at night, except a blind person, is an asshole.

Bar Etiquette

#4. Sexy people you'd like to sleep with. You'd like to sleep with them. Hence, free drinks for the sexy.

#5. Friends. Hey, they're your friends.

BTs have to be careful about free drinks because they can easily get out of hand. It doesn't take long to realize that a free drink usually results in a larger tip. The temptation to give away a lot of free drinks to pad your own wallet can be a strong one. A BT who takes this route can soon be giving away 20–30% of the drinks he pours, which results in a larger bottom line for him at the expense of the owner.

For this reason, most bars have a policy regarding free drinks, which can range from quite lenient to absolutely no free drinks at all. In establishments with a rule prohibiting free drinks, the BTs and servers are required to pay for any drinks they give away.

➤**People who don't get free drinks.** My rule of thumb is that people who expect a free drink don't get one, and that goes double for those who ask for a free drink. Stiffs, cheapskates and troublemakers don't get free drinks.

➤**Birthday drinks.** Free drinks for people on their birthdays isn't a hard-and-fast-rule. If someone is obviously wandering from bar to bar for free birthday drinks, and will leave as soon as they've finished their free one and aren't someone you'd want in your bar anyway, they don't get a free drink.

The way to get a free birthday drink is to first order a drink and leave a tip. Then, on your second round, mention that it's your birthday. Any BT will give you a free drink at this point, but be prepared to show your I.D..

►**Serviettes.** A.K.A. "Bev-naps" or "cocktail napkins" are used in most bars, primarily because they look more formal than simply setting the drink on the bare bar, and they also soak up the "bar-sweat" that forms on the sides of cold glasses and runs down them to form tiny puddles on the bar. However, in my opinion, the most important reason to use serviettes is that they cut down on spilled drinks. A person, especially one who is more than slightly drunk, is less likely to knock over a drink sitting on a serviette because the white square of paper is easily seen, even if only in peripheral vision.

►**Living above bars.** People who live above bars have to put up with noise. The reason that the apartment above a bar is for rent is probably that the previous tenants couldn't stand the noise. If you're thinking of moving in above a bar, you should consider this. If you look at the place during the day, it would be wise to come back at night to see what the noise level is. I have no sympathy for people who move in above a bar and then complain that it's too noisy. The bar was there before you were, and the world doesn't have to conform to your standards. Maybe you should consider moving to the suburbs. Cities are exciting places and sometimes excitement causes noise. If every neighborhood in the city were as quiet as a suburban neighborhood, it would be a boring city.

►**Hats in a bar.** Some bars don't allow men to wear hats inside. This isn't because they are sticklers for outdated manners but because hats can cause fights in certain crowds. What usually happens is some Gomer who's half-crocked thinks it would be fun to pluck the hat off a guy's head and try it on for size. It may amuse his buddies, but the guy who finds himself hatless takes exception to being the source of their

Bar Etiquette

amusement, belts the Gomer, and a fight ensues. This "no hats" rule is rare, though, and the bars that have it generally aren't worth going into anyway. For all other bars, men are not required to remove their hats upon entry and, unless you belong to the Art Deco Society or some such thing, it's not considered a breach of etiquette.

►**Shades in a bar.** Anyone except a blind person who wears shades in a bar at night is an asshole.

►**Lost and found.** Most bars have lost-and-founds, usually an out-of-the-way cubbyhole or drawer. If you lose something in a bar, you will have the best chance of retrieving it if you act as soon as possible after it's lost. The longer it stays, the less likely you are to get it back. The interpretation will be that the owner is either not interested in it or has forgotten where it was lost. Nine times out of ten, people who don't return for a lost item within twenty-four hours won't return at all, and nine times out of ten, items not claimed within forty-eight hours are no longer there to be claimed.

►**How to avoid losing valuables in a bar.** If you bring anything of value into a bar, keep it on your person at all times or you risk it being lost or stolen. Don't hang your purse over the back of your chair or barstool, don't leave your camera or wallet on the bar. If it's a large item, keep it in contact with your body so that if someone tries to steal it you will sense movement. Don't leave any garment on a coat rack or otherwise unattended. If you enter a bar during daylight hours wearing shades and take them off, put them in your pocket or purse immediately. People often remove their shades upon entering a bar and,

I got my customers drunk and they left me all this cool stuff.

Bar Etiquette

if they leave after it's dark, will forget that they had them until it's too late. It's a similar story for umbrellas during periods of intermittent showers; if you leave a bar after the rain has stopped there's a good chance you will forget that you had an umbrella with you until it resumes raining. Book bags and small backpacks are other items that people will put on the floor by their feet and leave behind when they go.

►**Finding money in a bar.** Generally I would advise a reasonable amount of honesty when it comes to finding valuables in a bar, but money on the floor is fair game. If you find a twenty on the floor and wave it around asking for the owner, then several are sure to show up. This isn't necessarily dishonesty on the part of your fellow patrons. People in bars spend money more quickly than they realize and may think that that's how they depleted their wad so quickly.

 My advice, if you see a bill on the ground, is to pick it up quickly and put it in your pocket. Don't stop to see what denomination it is, don't look around to see if anyone noticed. If people are milling around it and you don't want to attract attention and end up in an argument, you should remove your wallet from your pocket or purse and toss it next to or on top of the bill, then scoop them both up in one motion. Anyone who sees you will assume that the bill fell out when you dropped your wallet. You may also choose to turn the bill into the BT on duty, but if you do so, be advised that that bill is going directly into the tip jar.

►**How to avoid losing money in a bar.** Keep your money in a wallet and file the bills in order of denomination so you will have some idea of what you're pulling out even after you've had a few. Don't keep your money wadded up in your pocket, as pulling them out will often allow one or more to fall to the ground. Be especially careful as you approach the bar, because this is where most bills are dropped. In fact, if you're tapped-out, the best places to look for that twenty you need to extend your night are along the brass rail at the foot of the bar and in front of the service station.

If you lose your wallet you must act quickly. Notify the BT and retrace your steps. Try to imagine where the wallet could have been kicked by a passerby. People aren't all that observant, and your wallet may lie unnoticed for some time. Check the trash cans in the restrooms. People who find or steal a wallet will want to strip it of its cash as soon as possible, and they will want to do so unobserved. Once they have the money, they will want to dispose of the evidence. Because this person could be of either gender, both restrooms should be checked. Of course, your cash will be gone by the time you find your wallet in a trash can in the restroom, but at least you will have your wallet and I.D., etc.

►**Telephone.** Never use the bar phone without first asking the BT if it's okay. The bar phone is for bar business and personal calls should generally be made on the public phone, but sometimes the BT will let a customer, especially a regular, use the bar phone for a quick, local call. But don't presume this to be the case. Always ask first.

The above mentioned bar business includes calls from other BTs, the bar manager, the boss, distributors, prospective customers, and friends of customers. As I bartend at night, the calls I am most likely to receive are from the last two categories

Bar Etiquette

of callers. The business they wish to conduct runs in two primary veins: "Are you open?" and "Is so and so there and can you page him?" In the bar where I work no one has the time or interest in dealing with these calls, so the phone is unplugged and the answering machine takes over.

➤**Cellular phones.** These are a fact of modern life, but they can be a nuisance. A friend of mine refers to them as the gold chains of the '90's. Occasionally some slob with a big cigar will whip one out at the bar and start talking loudly into it, much to the annoyance of those around him. Apparently, they want to advertise the fact that they can afford one of these modern marvels, but you know what? No one cares. They're everywhere now. They're no big deal. Get over it. Use some sense. If you need to use your cell-phone, take it away from the bar to a quite corner where you can hear better and where your conversation won't annoy others.

➤**Calling cabs.** I don't like calling cabs. On weekends the cab companies are often busy and their phones are tied up, so I'm forced to stay on the phone for several minutes. This takes me away from my work and costs me money. Besides this, if the bar is on a busy street, it's faster to hail a cab than it is to call one.

What annoys me most is that when customers have the BT call a cab they often go out to the street to wait for it, then hedge their bets by attempting to hail one. They are usually successful, and when the cab arrives they have long since departed, leaving an angry cabby in the BT's face.

People don't seem to understand or care that cab drivers,

like BTs, are doing piecework: the more pieces of work they complete in a shift, the more money they make. On top of this, cabbies don't receive an hourly wage and must pay for the use of their cabs, so in essence they start out every shift in the hole. The first couple of hours they work goes to pay their "gate and gas," and only after that do they start making money. When you call a cab and don't wait for it, you've caused a cabby to drive from wherever he was to the location from which you ordered the cab, and he has received nothing for his work.

The way I've come to handle this problem is to first explain to the customer that it's faster to hail a cab on the street. If he insists on having me call a cab, I insist that he wait in the bar until the cabby comes inside. This doesn't always work, because in a busy bar it's difficult to keep track of customers, and they often sneak out to hail a cab. If I see them leave, I immediately call and cancel the cab.

Other BTs I've spoken with on this subject say that they require a five-dollar deposit from the customer, refundable when the cabby arrives. If the customer walks, the cabby gets the five bucks for his trouble. BTs who use this method say it works fairly well.

Of course, both of these systems can be circumvented by the customer calling a cab on a public phone, or from their cellular phone, and then hailing a cab on the street. The effect this has is that eventually cabs won't take calls from a bar that has had too many *dead calls*.

▶**Flyers.** Occasionally, some bonehead, trying to promote a new bar or club, will decide that another bar is the best place to find prospective customers. While this may be true, it

Bar Etiquette

doesn't follow that BTs are going to allow flyers, advertising their competition, to be handed out or otherwise distributed in their bars. Promoters engaging in this behavior can expect to hear from the BT. Any flyers left laying around will, most likely, be tossed directly into the trash can.

➤**Bar ecology.** Cutting down on waste is a concern in all sectors of modern life, and bars are no exception. For example, most bars these days separate their trash into bottles and other sorts of garbage. The reason for this isn't ecological awareness, it's economics. It costs money to have trash collected, and the charge is based on the volume that must be collected each week. Over half of all garbage generated by a bar consists of bottles, bars can cut down on their trash collection bill by a large percentage if they isolate their bottles and have them collected by recyclers, who charge nothing for their service because they plan to sell the bottles. Cardboard is another large component of the garbage generated in a bar, and it too can be collected by recyclers.

Customers can also help to cut down on waste. One way customers contribute to needless waste in a bar comes in the way that they deal with spills. When a customer spills a drink he will grab the nearest thing handy to wipe up the spill. This tends to be a large wad of serviettes. The best way to deal with spills is to use a bar rag, but I would advise that you ask a member of the staff first before grabbing a rag off the bar. Some bars have a low supply of clean bar rags, and BTs covet the clean, dry ones because they like to hang them on their apron string and use them to dry their hands in between washing glasses. A BT who is used to having a relatively clean bar rag in a bar where clean rags are at a premium will not like to see one of the clean ones used to wipe up a spill, especially a spill that's on the floor. If asked for a rag the BT will, most likely, produce a really grungy one from behind the bar. This is a rag that has already been cycled through its usage from the clean, dry one on his waist to the rolled or folded damp one on the bar, to its current position of filthy mess for wiping up spills on the floor.

In every bar there are usually two restrooms, and what goes on here often exceeds their intended uses. These excesses may include smoking, snorting and injecting drugs, taking baths, lover's quarrels, sexual encounters of various descriptions, changing clothes, etc. BTs prefer the use of these rooms to be confined to their intended use, but it's difficult to keep an eye on what goes on here because they are hidden away and often have locks on them, which is the reason they are chosen for the above activities in the first place. One way to keep these sorts of activities to a minimum is not to put a lock on the door. But then other

Nature's Call

problems arise: complaints from customers, primarily female, about the lack of privacy.

This concern over restrooms has nothing to do with prudishness and everything to do with the smooth operation of a bar. Remembering back to the 80's, when cocaine usage was rife in bars and clubs, it was nearly impossible to tend to nature due to the parties conducted in these tiny, private rooms. A long restroom line is not conducive to good business in a bar. Like the old saying goes, "You don't buy beer, you rent it," and people won't keep renting their beverage of choice if they can't make room for more.

►**Men vs. Women.** There are differences between the way men and women make use of the rooms set aside for them. Men's rooms smell worse. Maybe that's just my opinion because I'm a man and prefer the smell of women, but I think it has to do with the fact that men tend to miss the target, especially when they're drunk. Of course, to be fair, I must point out that it isn't easy to hit such a small target as a toilet bowl with a high pressure hose; that's why urinals were invented. Men also tend to spend a lot less time in this room. Washing hands and primping in the mirror is just a waste of time when there's all that beer to drink.

Women, on the other hand, seem to camp out in the women's room. They like to draw or write with lipstick on the mirror, and they seem to enjoy blotting their lipstick on the walls. They also use an enormous amount of toilet paper and hand towels. Women will come up to the bar and complain when the women's room runs out of toilet paper; men never do. At the end of the night when I'm cleaning up, the wastebasket in the men's room is rarely full, while the wastebasket in the women's room is always over-flowing onto the floor. This may indicate a greater ecological awareness on the part of men, but somehow I feel that's a misreading of the evidence.

Finally, there's the matter of the toilet seat. In the women's room it's always down, in the men's room it's always up. In bars that have mixed-use restrooms, this can be a source of annoyance for the female customers. To the males, I would say that you may want to think about putting the seat down when you're finished if there's a female next in line behind you. On the other hand, to the females, I would like to point out that if the seat is up when you enter, think of this as an assurance that the male before you didn't piss on it, because from what I've seen, rather than wasting time lifting the seat in a public restroom, men will simply piss over it and let the last few drops fall where they may. That's the reason toilet seats in public restrooms have a gap in the front; if they didn't, they would soon be corroded by the action of uric acid in that area where the last few drops are most likely to fall.

▶**Vomiting** This is another valid use of the restrooms, and as messy as it can be, due to the fact that people seem to be bad shots when blowing chunks, it is still preferable to other locations for this activity. Unfortunately, people see it otherwise. Perhaps it's due to lines at the restroom which preclude a timely entrance, or simply waiting until it's too late, but people will throw up just about anywhere in a bar: in a corner, in front of the restroom door, on the restroom door, on a wall, on the bar, on another customer, or on a member of the bar staff. I've never seen anyone throw up on the ceiling, but I've only been bartending for twelve years.

Bars are, among other things, places where people meet other people with whom they may form relationships. Many are strictly friendships, but many others are of the romantic nature. These can be of the opposite or same sex variety, but as I am writing this from the perspective of a BT in a primarily "straight" bar, it is the relationships of the male/female sort on which I will now comment.

►Men buying women drinks. From what I've seen I would advise that unless you know the woman in question, save your money. Men who buy strange women drinks, especially those who send drinks to women sitting at the other end of the bar with whom they have had no contact, are fools. Even fools get lucky, but generally you're just throwing your money away and making yourself the object of ridicule by the very woman you're trying to impress.

This practice can also cause problems for the BT, as some women will be offended by an unordered drink set before them, suspecting that the sender will feel he's earned her attention and will soon be moving over to talk with her. The way I deal with this is to ask the woman first if she wants the drink and to point out the fellow who is offering to buy it. If she says yes, I serve it; if not, I tell him that his offer was declined. This saves me the trouble of breaking up an uncomfortable situation later. Of course, there's always the joker who then insists that I serve her anyway. This is a guy who has more money then sense. My response to his insistence can be inferred from the section entitled **Who's in charge here?**

➤**Women buying men drinks.** This is the opposite of the situation outlined above, and is rare. Women do, of course, buy men drinks, but here we're talking about a case where the two people concerned have little, if any, previous contact. This situation doesn't present much possible trouble for the BT, and when I receive such a request I generally comply. Men usually find this flattering, because it's something that doesn't happen often. However, keep in mind that some men will interpret this sort of overture in the same way they would if they were the ones sending the drink: an invitation to sex. Not all men will read the situation this way, but the ones that do are the ones most likely to come scampering over to your side.

the Mating Game

►**Accepting drinks.** When someone sends you a drink in a bar, it's rarely just a drink they're sending; it's also a message that says "I want to meet you," or "I'm sitting here admiring you," or "I want to have sex with you," or "I'm lonely, talk to me," or "I have money to spend, are you impressed?," etc.

►**Men accepting drinks from women.** When a woman sends you a drink, you must remember that women are often more subtle in their approach to the mating game than men and often interpret signals differently than men. While this move is almost certainly an invitation to come over and talk with her, you would be well advised to approach her gingerly. If you swagger up acting as if sex is a foregone conclusion, you're likely to lose out. If you really botch it you could end up with a second free drink, the one you'll be wearing as you slouch back to your bar stool. The best approach is to walk over, thank her for the drink, and see where the ensuing conversation leads. Remember, she's the one who stuck her neck out and sent the message that she wanted to talk; now she wants to interview you. If you pass the test and sex is on her mind, she'll eventually make that clear.

►**Women accepting drinks from men.** If you have no interest in speaking with the man offering to buy you a drink, your best and most honest course of action is to decline it, because it's likely that soon after you've taken the first sip of that drink he'll be standing at your side chatting you up. Of course, you can take the position that if someone wants to buy you a drink that's his problem, that you can accept it and not owe him a thing. In other words, you can play dumb and act as if you believe that someone would give you

If men are more promiscuous than women, who are they promiscuous with?
N'art
FAST, CHEAP & EASY GRAPHICS
SINCE 1977
EXPLORE AND EXPLOIT

the Mating Game

something for nothing. This is a game I wouldn't advise playing, because it can often lead to more trouble than the drink is worth. I should add here that in such cases I am much less likely to intervene on behalf of the woman if she seems annoyed by the new source of attention she's receiving. My feeling is that she's the one who has caused the problem, and she can get herself out of it; that's the price of the "free" drink.

➤**BTs as sex objects.** It's no secret that BTs meet many members of the opposite sex or that they tend to be promiscuous. Why this is so is simply due to the nature of the job; BTs are the focal point of the bar because they're the ones you must go to for a drink, and thus they're accessible. Being the focus of what is essentially a party, it's as if the BT is on stage, which lends excitement to his persona. It also gives the person who is entertaining an interest in the BT certain important pieces of information—he is employed, and he is connected to a community in which he is an important and visible member, so he is not likely to be an ax-murderer. Plus, with a little bit of homework his schedule can be ascertained, so he is easy to find.

 On top of this, because a bar is a place where singles tend to congregate in the hopes of meeting other like-minded individuals, there is a high percentage of available members of the opposite sex in the bar at any given time, particularly in the evening. The fact that everyone in a bar is probably drinking alcohol, which lowers inhibitions as it heightens amorous ambitions, rounds out the picture. Given all this, it's easy to see why BTs, on average, aren't good choices for those seeking long-term relationships. The temptations are great, and while opportunity may knock but once, temptation will bang on the door for years.

➤**Amorous moods.** Occasionally two customers will decide that kissing one another would be a good idea. There's nothing wrong with this, up to a point. But when it goes on for longer than five or ten minutes and reaches the level of serious face sucking and body groping, it will begin to annoy those nearby.

➤**Coitus anyone?** On rare nights two customers will decide that sexual intercourse with one another, in a bar, is a good idea. This is never a good idea. I have seen couples pull it off with some amount of discretion but for the most part it's two people who are way too drunk to be out in public. It's time to go home, or at least to a motel.

➤**Nudity.** This is generally the domain of women, inebriated women who want to get attention by exposing prized body parts, usually breasts. Some will pretend they're doing a bar trick and affix matches to their nipples, which they then light on fire. Others use the ploy of showing off a tattoo that's in a private place. But most simply pull up their blouses and flash the bar.

This sort of behavior usually annoys the other women at the bar and earns the exhibitor a few admiring hoots from the menfolk, so it does work to that degree. But it also makes the woman in question the butt of a few jokes before everyone returns to what they were doing before. If she persists in this behavior the BT will generally put a stop to it because it can eventually lead to trouble if one or more of the simpler fellows in the bar feel her displays are meant to attract him to her side.

➤**Mating Season.** The mating season for humans begins on the 31st of October, Halloween, and runs until the 21st of December, the Winter Solstice. This is the period of the year in which couples are most likely to form.

Bars are social places. The social interaction that takes place therein, fueled by, and sometimes encumbered by alcohol generates arguments, disagreements and transgressions of various sorts. Occasionally these situations cross the line of acceptable behavior into the realm of harassment.

►Men harassing women. Overzealous men, often drunk and misreading signals, are the most frequent offenders. If a woman is being harassed by a male customer, it is important that she make this clear to the BT and to the man who is annoying her. Her best course of action is to consider moving to another area of the bar. If that isn't convenient, or if the man follows her, then she should let the offending party know that she would prefer to be left alone. If subtlety doesn't work, and it often doesn't, try a more direct approach, such as, "I'm tired of this conversation, go away." If that doesn't work, it's time to bring the BT into the picture. Once you've established the fact that this person is bothering you, the BT is in a much better position to help you.

Some women, when confronted with this situation, will continue to engage in polite conversation with the offending male while, at the same time, making pleading glances at the BT in hopes of an intervention. This puts the BT in the awkward position of seeming to make a value judgment of the situation; it personalizes the BT's involvement. This is especially true if the BT is a male, in which case he may be viewed by the offending male customer as a rival, perhaps one who is himself trying to make points with the woman. This is a bad situation, as it can lead to a physical confrontation, which is sometimes required in a BT's line of work but which, due to the possibility of physical injury and/or legal ramifications, is always best avoided.

If, on the other hand, the woman has clearly established the fact that she doesn't appreciate the attention of the offending male, the BT can then intervene as a neutral third party whose job it is to maintain order. The offending male may at this time direct a dirty look or a few choice words at the BT and/or the woman in an attempt to save face, but that's usually as far as it will go.

►**Women harassing men.** This is less common than the

Harassment

above situation, and less problematic, at least in terms of its ability to cause problems and disruptions. Occasionally, though, it does get out of hand, and can present some special problems, particularly if the BT is male. It just doesn't look good for a male BT to physically eject a woman customer. Additionally, you can't use the full range of force against a woman that you can against a man, and you generally don't have female customers (*i.e.* back-up) standing around waiting to get into a barroom brawl the way you do with male customers. You're pretty much on your own, limited to grabbing her arms and moving her towards the door as best you can, which is fine if you're bigger and stronger than she is, but if she's near your size and resorts to screaming, biting, and kicking, it can get ugly.

There is another form of female on male harassment which takes place when a woman feigns sexual interest in a man, either for her own ego gratification, to get a free drink or, more cruelly, for the entertainment of herself and/or her friends. This is a far more subtle and intractable situation for the BT. For one thing, society allows for a wide range of behavior in this area, so long as there is no physical contact or other physically violent actions. The BT who suspects trouble is forced to make a value judgement, knowing that he could be wrong (perhaps the woman really does have an interest in this fellow) or to simply ignore it and hope he is wrong. This behavior is potentially as dangerous as other forms of harassment. For instance, if she plays this game with more than one male, or if the BT gets mixed up in it, a fight may result.

The bottom line; troublesome females are no more welcome in bars than the troublesome males.

►**Men harassing men.** An argument over a woman, an argument over nothing at all; what ever the reason this situation requires quick attention by the BT so that it doesn't escalate to the point where a physical intervention is required. While the same rules apply here as in other cases of harassment, this situation can quickly deteriorate to a point where reason has no effect. This is especially true when the two fellows involved have a strongly developed sense of masculine propriety. If separating the two individuals by way of reason fails, and an altercation seems imminent, the BT will generally take a quick inventory of the available muscle in the room and direct it to the problem in the hopes of averting a fight or, if one is already underway, to break it up. The persons responsible for the disruption will often be ejected, regardless of who "started it". People who fight in bars are a lot more trouble than they're worth.

►**Women harassing women.** This usually remains on the verbal level. "Cat fights" are rare in my experience, at least since I left high school. Some men claim they enjoy a good cat fight. I would guess that the phenomenon of female mud wrestling gets its appeal from this fascination with women fighting women. If I can remember correctly from my days in high school, I believe this interest stems from the possibility of one or both of the contestants being partially disrobed during the heat of battle. While I'll confess to a healthy interest in partially disrobed females, I prefer to witness them without the benefit of other spectators and under somewhat calmer conditions.

Harassment

►**Customers harassing the BT.** This ranges from the annoying yakety-yak of drunks, repeating their stories endlessly, to outright hostility. In the case of drunks and other boring people the BT will escape by finding other work to do, or if it's slow rely on occasional head nodding and uttering "yeah…yeah" at appropriate intervals. Hostile customers simply get cut off and shown the door.

►**Customers harassing the Cocktail waitress.** Many men are attracted to cocktail waitresses. This is partially due to the fact that cocktail waitresses are women in a bar who appear to be alone. They are also generally attractive women, as bar owners know that an attractive woman will hold the attention of male customers longer than an unattractive one. Attractive women, all other things being equal, will generally make more money per shift than plain ones, because male customers will order from them more often and tip them better in an attempt to get their attention and to impress them.

  On the other hand, these women aren't necessarily there to meet men, but to make a living. Some waitresses who aren't interested in advances from male customers will wear a fake wedding ring to advertise themselves as off-limits, but as this is fairly common knowledge, men will often ignore wedding rings on waitresses. What these men fail to grasp is that while these women may not be married, they are, by wearing the ring, signifying that they aren't interested in advances from male customers. It's worth mentioning here that one of the quickest ways to get yourself ejected from a bar is to insult, touch, pinch or otherwise harass a cocktail waitress.

Experienced BT's check out each new customer as they enter the bar. This isn't always possible, as BT's are often concerned with various tasks, but other factors permitting, they will check you out. The reason for this is that they want to know who's in their bar and to be ready for trouble before trouble is ready for them.

What they're looking for is anyone who stands out from the crowd, anyone who looks angry or otherwise disturbed, anyone who has caused trouble in the past. If they see someone they suspect of being a potential problem they will alert the other BT's so they can all check him out until he's deemed no threat.

Troublemakers

Some problems are apparent from the get-go:

➤ **A person who's been 86'd, a homeless person, anyone selling anything, an obviously deranged or drunk or drugged person, someone with an animal or a child, someone with a bicycle or an enormous backpack.**

Others are less apparent, but here are some tipoffs:

➤**People who wander slowly about the room but make no attempt to buy a drink or locate friends,** particularly if they are carrying a newspaper. This is the M.O. of a sneak thief looking for an unattended purse, wallet, or cash. The newspaper is used to hide the loot as he takes to the street.

➤**People who go in and out of the bar repeatedly.** This behavior is often associated with drugs; either the sale, purchase, or use thereof. In bars that enforce the California no-smoking law, these people are now often lost in the tide of smokers; going out to smoke, coming back in to drink.

➤**A person who announces that he hasn't had a drink in a year (or any long span of time).** What is implied in this announcement is that this person has a drinking problem and has been forced to quit. However, he has now decided to fall off the wagon and has chosen your bar in which to do it. Lucky you.

➤**People who hop from table to table talking to strangers.** This could be someone trying to buy or sell drugs or it could just be an annoying person. Either way, he's not good for the bar.

➤**People who make those around them nervous or uncomfortable.**

➤**People especially sullen or taciturn.**

➤**People who are overly animated.**

➤**People who act overly friendly to perfect strangers.**

➤**People that order a drink, then complain that it's no good or too expensive.**

➤**People who appear to be affiliated with gangs, sports teams, fraternities, or the military,** particularly if they enter as a group.

➤**People who exhibit bizarre behavior.**

➤**People far younger or far older than the average age group that frequents the bar.**

➤**People who appear to be far below or far above the average income level of those who frequent the bar.**

➤**People who arrive in stretch-limos.**

The above tipoffs are not definite indicators of trouble-makers, but they are indicators of possible trouble and most BT's will keep an eye on them until their suspicions are proved wrong.

Each person should be given the benefit of the doubt; it can cause considerable trouble and embarrassment to all involved if a BT acts prematurely on his assumptions and they're proved faulty. There's a fine line between acceptable and unacceptable behavior in a bar. Bars are places where there is going to be what would be considered aberrant behavior in other settings but which must be expected and tolerated to a degree. To what degree varies from bar to bar and from BT to BT. Reading people, assessing situations that arise between people, making a judgment call as to when the line of acceptable behavior has been crossed and by whom, and then dealing effectively and fairly with the situation is the most difficult part of bartending.

Occasionally, customers or even bar staff will, due to poor judgment, absence of mind, or drunkenness, do things which put themselves and/or others in danger. Beyond simply not wanting to see someone get hurt, there are legal ramifications: persons hurt on bar premises can and will sue for damages. Courts generally err on the side of the plaintiff, even if the plaintiff admits to being drunk, because the bar and the BT are considered responsible for creating the drunken state in the first place. Below are some of the more common hazards.

▶**Putting empty glassware where it shouldn't be.** Customers deposit glasses wherever they happen to be standing at the time their glasses become empty. This can be dangerous when the glass is left in a place where someone can step on it. For instance, in the bar where I work there is a stairway that leads to the public phone. When the bar is crowded, customers occasionally sit on the stairway for a few minutes. If they finish a drink while sitting there, they leave the empty glass on the steps. The possibility for an accident is great in this case, as the glass is not easily seen by a customer descending the stairway. If a customer steps on it he may take a tumble, with cuts and broken bones as the result. A more common place for empty glassware is on the floor near the wall. This isn't nearly as dangerous, but can also cause an injury if someone steps on it.

▶**Putting full glassware where it shouldn't be.** Customers aren't as likely to abandon a full glass as an empty one, but it does happen, and can be just as dangerous. They will sometimes place a drink near the edge of a table, where it can be knocked off onto the floor. An additional danger created by full glassware is the contents, which, when spilled on the floor, can create a slipping hazard for other customers.

▶**Putting customers where they don't belong.** Sometimes customers will get up on a barstool, tabletop, or even the bar itself. There are bars that not only allow this sort of behavior but encourage it. They tend to be bars that cater to what I call the "post-frat" crowd, or what is more commonly referred to as Yuppies. All too often this crowd has proven that their imbecilic behavior has no boundaries, so that they find this an endlessly amusing stunt doesn't surprise me.

Dangerous Behavior

What does surprise me is that a BT, even a bar manager or the bar owner, can allow or even encourage behavior that portends a massive lawsuit that hinges on the grace of a drunk in high heels and a tight skirt on a wet bar littered with glassware and flanked on one side by bottles and bartenders and on the other side by glassware and customers. The fact that they put up with this from the crowd most likely to bring a lawsuit in the event of an accident, and most able to afford the best ambulance-chaser money can buy, absolutely dumfounds me. But maybe I'm just a worrywart: I've never heard of one of these bars having such a lawsuit brought against them. Then again, maybe I'm out of the loop on this one, or maybe it's a matter of the odds catching up with them. One can only hope.

➤**Dancing.** If there's room for it, fine, but in crowded bars dancing can present a hazard, because customers and servers must negotiate the tight spaces between people in the bar. Flying glassware is often the result of dancing in tightly packed bars.

➤**Animals.** It's against the Health Code, but that's the least of the problems associated with animals in a bar. Animals, and dogs are the primary offenders, don't belong in bars. But dog-owners love to bring their pets with them. They will assure you that their dog wouldn't hurt a fly. Then someone inadvertently steps on or kicks the animal and it reflexively bites a customer. Or, the dog finds a comfortable place to lie down, which just happens to be in the path of an inebriated customer who trips over the animal. The owner's assurances of safety leave with them and their chattel and the bar is stuck with a lawsuit.

►**Children.** Occasionally, customers will want to bring a child, usually a very young child, with them into a bar. Their reasoning is that an infant obviously isn't going to be drinking, and that no A.B.C. agent or cop would bust a bar for an under aged customer in such a case, and that may be true. The problem is that bars can be dangerous places for adults, so they will be even more so for infants. The possible scenarios are too numerous and horrifying to list here, but suffice it to say that children don't belong in bars.

►**Pyrotechnics.** People like to play with fire. There are bar tricks based on matches and Zippos. People like to burn things and even to light their drinks on fire. A certain amount of this behavior is to be expected and tolerated, but it's wise to keep it below the level of bonfires. Firecrackers and stink bombs are as good a reason to expel a patron from a bar as they were to expel a student from grade school, where they most likely developed this hobby. Lighting fellow customers on fire is considered bad form in most bars.

➤**Barroom bets.** If you spend any time in a bar, you will eventually meet someone who will offer to bet you that he or she can do something that you know is impossible. My advice is to never bet more than it's worth to you to see just how this person will accomplish the feat, because you're going to lose.

Generally speaking, these bets will be based on the person's ability to perform seemingly impossible physical acts. Sometimes it's based on a trick, sometimes it's based on ambiguous wording or esoteric knowledge, but no matter how impossible the act seems, I assure you that the person making the claim can do it.

These bets can usually be brought down in price from five dollars to a drink to nothing but a challenge. Essentially, these people just want to show you that they know something you don't know or that they can do something you can't do. They'll take your money if you're foolish enough to bet them, but when pushed, and if there are no takers, they will usually perform their little trick for free.

►**Sucker bets.** Though often used interchangeably with "barroom bets," I define "sucker bets" a bit differently. I see these as more predatory and having less to do with tricks or feats and more to do with cons. They are often based on some sort of information or trivia. As they have little to do with showing off, they almost always involve a bet, and the person pushing for the bet definitely wants your money.

A good rule of thumb is not to place bets in bars. For one thing, if you're in a bar you're probably drinking, and your mind won't be as clear as it should be for wagering. Men seem to be particularly vulnerable, as alcohol heightens machismo and challenges are hard to walk away from under these circumstances. Here, just as with "barroom bets," if someone claims something is so, no matter how ridiculous and unlikely it seems, you can be sure it probably is so, and you will lose your money if you bet.

►**Bar tricks.** People who spend a lot of time in bars often amuse themselves and their friends with games and tricks that can be played with the things you find around a bar: napkins, matches, glasses, spoons, knives, etc. Betting usually isn't part of these diversions, and while some are quite boring others can be ingenious.

The best one I remember was shown to me by a drop-in customer. After a couple of drinks and a bit of conversation with me and a person seated next to her at the bar, she asked me for two highball glasses and a knife. She told me to hold the two glasses underwater in my sink until they were full and there were no air

Tricksters

bubbles inside them. Then she told me to put the tops together with the rims aligned and remove them slowly from the sink, one right side-up, the other upside-down. I did so and, due to the vacuum created by the absence of air, the water remained inside the two-part vessel.

She then had me place them on the bar. She put a dime on the top of the two-part vessel (the bottom of the upside-down glass), laid the knife next to the glasses and told me that the object was to get the dime inside the bottom glass without spilling any water from the top glass, and that I could use nothing but the knife to touch the glasses or the dime. I looked at the problem for a while but could think of no solution, and figuring there had to be a trick to it, I gave up and waited to see how she would solve it.

Her first move was to take the knife and gently tap the upper glass until it slid over slightly. There was now a gap between the rims of the upper and lower glasses. The vacuum inside plus, perhaps, the surface tension of the water, prevented any of the liquid from leaking out through the thin opening.

Then she took the knife and pushed the dime from where it was lying in the center of the upside-down glass to a position where it overhung the edge of the upside-down glass, enabling her to slide the knife under the dime. In this way she was able to pick up the dime and lower it into position next to the lip of the lower glass. She turned the knife to the side, which allowed the dime to slide off the knife and through the gap between the rims of the glasses. The dime slid through the water and came to rest in the bottom of the upright glass. She then tapped the upper glass back into place. Problem solved.

►**Barroom cons.** Never buy jewelry from a guy you meet in a bar, no matter how sad his story is or how much he tries to convince you it's stolen merchandise.

A shot of booze will reach the rim of a snifter when turned on it's side.

Is the glass half empty, or half full? You decide.

Optimist

The glass is half full. My reason for believing this has as much to do with my outlook on life as it does with the simple query about the status of a glass of wine. I feel that a positive attitude will ultimately result in a positive outcome. Due to this basic belief I can only view this glass of wine as being half full. To see the glass as half full gives one hope for the future, and hope is all we really have in this life; it's what Pandora was able to salvage from the disastrous situation when her curiosity was tempted by a cruel god. Poor Pandora! But her suffering was not in vain, not so far as I'm concerned, for I, just as Pandora, retain hope in this often cruel and confusing world. For me the glass will always be half full. If more people thought this way the world would be a better place.

Pessimist

The glass is half empty. When one encounters a vessel which contains a volume of liquid equal to half of it's capacity what is one to assume about it's status? Is one to assume that someone has filled the glass halfway, then left it sitting and will return at some later date to finish the job? Or does one assume that someone has filled the glass, drank their fill and then left the glass sitting? Those who are of the former view are those who routinely quit before a job is finished; how else could they believe someone has aborted, at midpoint, the simple task of filling a glass with wine? The latter position is not only the more likely one, it's the position which engenders a mental state geared toward getting the job done. It's the only position a responsible person can take.

Answer: both are incorrect; this is a full wine glass.

appendix i

Is the Glass Half-Empty or Half-Full?

Customers occasionally feel the BT has under-poured their drinks. Below is a brief and general guide to how full a glass should be.

➤**Shot.** A shot glass should be filled to the rim.

➤**Rocks.** A rocks glass should be filled within a quarter inch of the rim unless it is being used to serve booze neat, then it should be about half full. BTs will often use a rocks glass to serve booze neat because it's more convenient to drink from than a shot glass filled to the rim.

➤**Highball.** Highballs should be filled to within a quarter inch of the rim. Exceptions to this are:

Margaritas with salted rims or salty dogs. With these drinks its best to leave a little extra room so the salt won't dissolve into the drink. The BT achieves this lower level by adding less ice to the glass, not by adding less booze, so you aren't being cheated.

Booze over. Some bars serve booze over in a highball glass for the same reason they serve neat shots in rocks glasses; it gives the customer extra room to slosh their drinks around without spilling them (this practice of serving drinks in the next largest glass is sometimes referred to as serving it in a "nervous" glass). Booze over in a highball glass should be slightly over half full.

➤**Martini.** This will vary, depending on the size of the glass. Some bars use over-sized martini glasses (Approximately six ounces) and pour their martinis an inch short of the rim. Others use tiny martini glasses (Approximately three ounces) and the glass is filled to the rim. An averaged sized martini glass is four ounces and should be filled to within a quarter inch of the rim. One thing to remember about martini glasses is that they are inverted cones, and as such, the volume of each ascending cross section of the glass holds more than the preceding cross section, in other words, the top half of the glass holds three times as much as the bottom half. Knowing this, you can see that what might seem like a huge martini might just be a huge martini glass, filled to within an inch of the rim.

Another thing to consider is the garnish. If you order two martinis, one with an olive and one with a twist the one with the olive will appear fuller because the olive displaces more volume than the twist.

➤**Wine.** Wine glasses should be filled just over halfway to the rim.

➤**Beer.** A pint of tap beer should have a 1/2"-3/4" head of foam.

➤**Snifters.** A shot of cognac in a snifter will leave mostly empty space in the glass. The way to check the pour is to lay the snifter on its side. If there's a full shot of booze it should reach to the rim.

appendix ii

Types of Glasses

Not all bars have a full complement of glassware. Many will put one type of glass to two or more uses. The reasons for this are: (1) Cost. It costs more to have more types of glassware; and (2) Space. There often isn't enough space to have all the different types of glassware called for by the writers of bar guides. Usually a bar will have the most room behind the bar allotted to the types of glassware it uses most: rocks, highball and beer glasses, for instance. Infrequently used glassware must fit into the remaining space. If there isn't room for a type that is almost never needed, the bar will choose to do without and press another type of glass into service when the need arises.

➤**Shot.** These are the smallest glasses in the bar. They hold an ounce and a half of liquor. Shot glasses often have a white line painted just below the rim to indicate one ounce.

➤**Rocks.** This is the little glass, generally holding four ounces, that you get when ordering booze on the rocks or neat.

➤**Highball.** These glasses look like rocks glasses only larger (six or eight ounces).

➤**Collins** (also called Chimney, Zombie or Tall). These are the tall thin glasses that Collins and other tall drinks come in.

➤**Pint.** The biggest glass in most bars, used for serving tap beer.

➤**Pilsner.** Slender, tapered beer glass with a heavy footing.

➤**Martini.** These are the inverted cones with stems that "up" drinks come in.

➤**Champagne flute.** These are the glasses that champagne is served in. They are shaped like long, thin, tapered cylinders and are stemmed.

➤**Wine glass.** Rounded sides, stemmed.

➤**Snifter.** Squat, round, stemmed. For cognac or aged single-malt scotch.

➤**Coffee or bell.** Shaped like an upside-down bell and stemmed. For drinks that use coffee or hot water as an ingredient.

appendix iii

Bar Terms

➤**Back-bar.** The large fixture against the wall behind the bar where the *call* and *top-shelf* booze, the glassware, and the cash register are kept. They range from simple and utilitarian to extremely ornate. The ornate ones are highly prized and will often be bought from old bars that are going out of business to do service in a bar that's being built or remodeled.

➤**Bump or up-charge.** An extra charge for certain drinks such as *up* drinks, coffee drinks and *tall* drinks.

➤**Call.** These are the moderately priced name brands. They are a step up from *well*. They are usually found behind the BT, in the shelves below the back-bar.

They're called *call* because you must specify or call them by name. Otherwise, you'll get *well* booze.

➤**Dash.** This is the smallest amount in a drink recipe. Generally, it comes from a bottle with a tiny hole in the top, such as bitters. To pour a *dash* the BT takes the bottle and turns it over very quickly so just one squirt comes out.

➤**Double.** This indicates you want two *shots* (three ounces) of booze (four ounces in the case of Martinis, Old Fashioneds, and other drinks based on two-ounce pours).

➤**Float.** Booze added last and allowed to float on top of the drink. Roughly equal to a *one count*.

➤**Highball.** These are the mixed drinks most often ordered and consist of one *shot* of booze over ice in a highball glass filled with the appropriate mixer. Examples of *highballs* are, "gin and tonic," "Cape Cod," "rum and Coke," etc.

➤**Ice well.** This is the sink-like bin that the ice is kept in.

➤**In the weeds.** When the customers' demand for drinks exceeds the bar staff's ability to supply them.

➤**Neat.** This is how you order when you want booze straight from the bottle into your glass with no other modification and no ice. You can also say *straight* but *neat* is the more correct term.

➤**One-count.** Approximately one quarter of a *shot*.

➤**Pony shot.** One ounce of booze.

➤**Proof.** One-half of one percent of alcohol. Eighty-proof booze is forty percent alcohol.

➤**Rocks/over.** This means a *shot* of booze in a glass filled with ice.

➤**Shot or jigger.** One-and-a-half ounces of booze.

➤**Slammed.** When the customers' demand for drinks equals the bar staff's ability to supply them.

➤**Speed pour.** Using bottles fitted with pour spouts, BTs count in their heads at a regular rate to time their pour. It's faster than measuring with a shot glass and more accurate than eyeballing it.

➤**Speed well or speed rack.** This is the rack attached to the *ice well*. The BT stands behind it and is thus able to scoop ice into a glass and quickly grab a bottle from the well to produce a drink.

➤**Splash.** This means a *shot* of booze and a tiny amount of whatever you specify, for instance, "scotch with a *splash* of water," "gin with a *splash* of tonic," or "vodka with a *splash* of cranberry." It's used for mixers which are on the gun or in a bottle that don't take a *speed-pour* spout. These mixers can't be poured as accurately as booze from a *speed-pour* spout. A *splash* is roughly equivalent to a *one-count*.

➤**Stiff (stiffed).** A customer who doesn't tip (to serve a customer and receive no tip).

➤**Stirred vs. shaken.** The two ways booze is chilled. Both begin by putting ice into a mixing vessel and then adding booze. Then the BT either stirs the booze and ice with a long handled spoon or covers the mixing vessel and shakes it. Both methods chill the booze, and if it's a drink with two or more ingredients, mix them. Shaking is the more violent method and will generally make the booze colder quicker but will also dilute the drink more and often leave ice chips in the finished drink. In the case of gin it can also dissipate some of the fragrance. This is known as "bruising the gin," and some martini aficionados insist on stirred martinis.

➤**Tall.** When you order a drink *tall* you get the same amount of booze, a *shot*, but you get it in a Collins glass. The extra space in

Bar Terms

the glass is taken up by mixer, not by booze. You should order your drink *tall* if you want it to be more diluted. If you want it less diluted, you should order it with a *splash*. If you want more booze you should order a *double*, but remember, *doubles* cost twice as much as singles.

►**The gun.** A hose with a multi-buttoned nozzle for dispensing mixers such as cola, tonic, water, etc. It is used because it is faster, cheaper and easier than using bottled mixers.

►**Top-shelf.** These are the priciest offerings. They are called *top-shelf* because they are usually found on the shelves on top of the back-bar.

►**Up also straight-up.** This means chilled over ice (stirred or shaken), then strained into a glass, generally a chilled martini glass. Most *up* drinks are based on two-ounce pours rather than an ounce-and-a-half.

►**Virgin.** A drink without booze, for instance, a "virgin" Bloody Mary: tomato juice and all the garnishes but no vodka.

►**Well.** The entry-level booze, the cheap stuff you get if you don't order a name brand. They're called *well* because they're kept in the *speed well*. In upscale bars they are referred to as *house brands*.

►**Wilted drinks.** Drinks are said to be *wilted* when they pass their peak in terms of flavor. *Up* drinks *wilt* the fastest; that is, they become warmer than is preferred. For instance, a gin martini is only good for about twenty minutes after it's been made. *Over* drinks last a good deal longer; they are considered *wilted* when the ice has melted enough to dilute the drink past what is preferable. Beer *wilts* when it sits so long as to become too warm to drink.

►**86'd.** Bar terminology for a person who is no longer allowed on the premises. It also refers to an item that has run out and for which there is no replacement. For instance, if a keg of beer blows and there is no backup keg, that beer is said to be *86'd.*